a director prepares

●●● 'I am interested in the artistic process. In order to approach the theatre as artists, we should have a good look at our tools and how we make decisions. How do we approach one another in the arena of a rehearsal or on a stage? How do we begin, how do we proceed, and what are our allies?'

From the Introduction

●●● *A Director Prepares* is a fascinating and thought-provoking examination of the challenges of making theatre. In it, Anne Bogart speaks candidly and with immense wisdom of the courage required to create 'art with great presence'.

●●● Each chapter tackles one of the seven major areas Bogart has identified as both potential partner and potential obstacle to art-making. They are Violence; Memory; Terror; Eroticism; Stereotype; Embarrassment; and Resistance. Each one can be used to generate extraordinary creative energy, if we know how to use it.

●●● *A Director Prepares* offers every practitioner an extraordinary insight into the creative process. It is a handbook, bible and manifesto, all in one. No other book on the art of theatre comes even close to offering this much understanding, experience and inspiration.

Anne Bogart is Artistic Director of the SITI Company, which she founded with Tadashi Suzuki in 1992. She is Associate Professor at Columbia University.

a director prepares

seven essays on art and theatre

Anne Bogart

Routledge
Taylor & Francis Group

LONDON AND NEW YORK

First published 2001
by Routledge
11 New Fetter Lane, London EC4P 4EE

Simultaneously published in the USA and Canada
by Routledge
29 West 35th Street, New York, NY 10001

Reprinted 2002, 2003 (twice)

Routledge is an imprint of the Taylor & Francis Group

© 2001 Anne Bogart

Designed and Typeset in Melior and Scala Sans
by Keystroke, Jacaranda Lodge, Wolverhampton

Printed and bound in Great Britain by TJ International Ltd,
Padstow, Cornwall

British Library Cataloguing in Publication Data
A catalogue record for this book is available from the British Library

Library of Congress Cataloging in Publication Data
A catalogue record for this book has been requested

ISBN 0–415–23831–5 (hbk)
ISBN 0–415–23832–3 (pbk)

For my mother,
Margaret Spruance Bogart

contents

acknowledgements

I would like to thank my directing students at Columbia University for provoking these stories and opinions. Thanks also to the SITI Company who can transform theory into vital stage moments. And thanks to Jocelyn Clarke, Charles Mee, John Maloney, Carolyn Anderson, Wilma Hall, Sabine Andreas, Tina Landau and Talia Rodgers. A special thanks goes to Jon Jory for his insistence upon the necessity of this book. And finally, thanks to the Guggenheim Foundation who made the final stages of this book possible.

An earlier version of Chapter 4, 'Terror', first appeared in Anne Bogart, *Viewpoints*, published by Smith and Kraus (1995).

introduction

● ● ● Art is large and it enlarges you and me. To a shrunk-up world its
vistas are shocking. Art is the burning bush that both shelters and
makes visible our profounder longings.

(Jeanette Winterson)

I regard the theatre as an art form because I believe in its
transformative power. I work in the theatre because I want
the challenge of decisiveness and articulation in my daily
life. Directing chose me as much as I chose it. We found one
another. I like to watch. I like to study. I like to meet people
in the charged atmosphere of a rehearsal room or in a
theatre.

The theatre has been good to me. It has produced great
friendships, love, travel, hard work, fun, terror and pleasure.
It has also offered an entire life of study. Study is a full-
time engagement which includes reading books, reading
people, reading situations, reading about the past and

reading the present. To study, you enter into a situation with your whole being, you listen and then begin to move around inside it with your imagination. You can study every situation you are in. You can learn to read life while life is happening.

A scuba diver lies first in the water and waits until the entire ocean floor below starts to teem with life. Then the swimmer begins to move. This is how I study. I listen until there is movement and then I begin to swim.

I wanted to approach the theatre as an artist does, so I began to study the tools we have inherited and the procedures we use to make work in the theatre. I also studied how artists in other fields do what they do – how they think and how they create. I looked for helpful allies in the artistic process. How do we approach one another in the arena of a rehearsal or on a stage? How do we begin and then how do we go on?

As a director in the theatre I have encountered certain consistent problems that just do not go away. I have found myself repeatedly face to face with issues about violence, memory, terror, eroticism, stereotype, embarrassment and resistance. Rather than avoiding these problems I have found it fruitful to study them. And this study has changed the way I approach all my work in the theatre. The problems became allies.

This book is an articulation of this study.

Artists are individuals willing to articulate in the face of flux and transformation. And the successful artist finds new shapes for our present ambiguities and uncertainties.

The artist becomes the creator of the future through the violent act of articulation. I say violent because articulation is a forceful act. It demands an aggressiveness and an ability to enter into the fray and translate that experience into expression. In the articulation begins a new organization of the inherited landscape.

My good friend the writer Charles L. Mee, Jr helped me to recognize the relationship between art and the way societies are structured. He suggested that, as societies develop, it is the artists who articulate the necessary myths that embody our experience of life and provide parameters for ethics and values. Every so often the inherited myths lose their value because they become too small and confined to contain the complexities of the ever-transforming and expanding societies. In that moment new myths are needed to encompass who we are becoming. These new constructs do not eliminate anything already in the mix; rather, they include fresh influences and engender new formations. The new mythologies always include ideas, cultures and people formerly excluded from the previous mythologies. So, deduces Mee, the history of art is the history of inclusion.

National and international cultures as well as artistic communities are currently undergoing gigantic shifts in mythology. Technological and corporate revolutions have already changed the way we communicate, interact, live, make art and articulate our ethics and values. The myths of the last century are now inadequate to encompass these new experiences. We are living in the space between mythologies. It is a very creative moment, brimming with possibilities of new social structures, alternate paradigms and for the inclusion of disparate cultural influences.

I believe that the new mythologies will be created and articulated in art, in literature, architecture, painting and poetry. It is the artists who will create a livable future through their ability to articulate in the face of flux and change.

And yet, to succeed in this fast-changing world requires action, speed, decisiveness and hard work. To survive, to keep up, to feed a family, to ensure a roof over our heads, it is necessary to act from a very particular personal impulse: the survival instinct. And there is always the danger that this survival mode will dominate the artistic process. Most of the choices that we make in the survival mode issue from a need for security and advancement. But the instinct for security gives access only to a small part of our creative abilities. If we limit our impulses to the survival instinct, our scope and range of artistic work will be limited.

Lewis Hyde in his book entitled *The Gift: Imagination and the Erotic Life of Property* suggests that humans always take action and make decisions from two possible sources: the survival instinct or the gift-giving impulse.

The gift-giving impulse, like the survival instinct, also demands action and decisiveness, but the results differ because the intention that provokes the action has nothing to do with security. The action originates in the impulse to give someone a gift and the urge to create a journey for others outside of their daily experience. This instinct requires generosity, interest in others, and empathy.

Imagine planning a surprise birthday party for a friend. You make decisions about whom to invite and how to astonish and when to reveal, all with a sense of vicarious pleasure and excitement. You are structuring a journey for another person through direct empathy and feeling. The creative action and choices spring from the gift-giving impetus. This kind of impulse also determines how we compose a song, develop a story, design a house and, ideally, how we rehearse a play. We create journeys for others to be received in the spirit of a gift.

To approach the theatre as an art form we must be able to act in this empathetic spirit. But in our new global environment we find ourselves immersed in commerce, in the marketplace and, perhaps because of it, we find ourselves in conflict. In a world of commodities, we are not solely artists, but producers as well. Each of us is a producer and an artist in one and we must take care that one does not overwhelm the other. The producer in us must protect the gift giver and know when and how to give it space and freedom. The gift giver must step aside for the survival instinct in the right moments. The two must have their range and autonomy. How can we survive in the marketplace and still make art? How can we live in this fast and competitive environment and still walk into a rehearsal able to call upon the wild, violent child in us that makes the art poetic and magnificent and dangerous and terrifying? How can we, in a climate racing for survival, generate gifts with presence and generosity?

The study of violence, memory, terror, eroticism, stereotype, embarrassment and resistance has helped me to treat

5
●

each one as an ally in the creative process. It has been a journey outward towards other cultures, ideas and people. It has given me the courage to welcome the imbalance of our present uncertainties and attempt the violence of articulation in order to actualize the new mythologies of our time.

preface

story and anti-story

● ● ● Examine for a moment an ordinary mind on an ordinary day. The mind receives a myriad impressions – trivial, fantastic, evanescent, or engraved with the sharpness of steel. From all sides they come, an incessant shower of innumerable atoms; and as they fall, as they shape themselves into the life of Monday or Tuesday, the accent falls differently from of old; the moment of importance came not here but there.

(Virginia Woolf)

As a young man, the French philosopher Jean-Paul Sartre served as a sailor on a trading ship. One cold and stormy night the ship put into the port of Hamburg, Germany. Sartre got off the ship and made his way through the rainy wind-swept streets to the shelter of a seedy bar. He sat down at a table and ordered a drink. After a while a beautiful woman made her way towards his table, introduced herself and sat down next to him. They began to talk. Finally, after quite some time, the woman excused herself to go to the bathroom. As he sat alone, anticipating her return, Sartre imagined the night that he and the woman would spend together in a hotel room, the seduction, the sex, and ultimately their farewell the next morning. He imagined the letters they would send to one another in anticipation of reunion. He envisioned the story that lay ahead of them. Suddenly, as he awaited her return from the bathroom, Sartre experienced an epiphany. He realized that every moment of his life, including this one, offered a choice. He could either choose to live his life in the fabricated fiction of a story, or to embrace the discontinous blips and bleeps of human existence and live without the security of a story. All at once Sartre made the decision. He stood up and walked out of the bar and into the storm and never saw the woman again.

This preface is an attempt to organize the discontinuous blips and bleeps of my life into a story in order to create a context for reading this book. Ultimately though, like the Sartre episode, it is an anti-story. Reality is a construct of thought that desires continuity. Actually, the expectation of continuity is a glorious fiction. Reality depends upon our choices of what and how we choose to observe. The moments of my life are discontinuous and jump.

My father, Gerard S. Bogart, served for thirty years in the US Navy. He attained the rank of Captain. My mother's father was also in the Navy. His name was Admiral Raymond Ames Spruance and through his extraordinary ability as a strategist he is credited by many naval historians as a major catalyst in winning the battle of Midway during the Second World War. Typical of most military families, my family, including two brothers, my parents and I, moved every year or two to a new naval base in a different part of the United States or the world. This pattern of short whirlwind chunks of living reinforced something I later found in the theatre. Somewhere in every big, unfamiliar school I could always find a site of grace where plays were staged. These productions were quick, intense experiences where everybody got close, worked hard towards something wonderful and then later said good-bye for ever. I worked backstage on these productions. I scoured the hallways for props during classes. I took notes for the teacher/director. I stayed late and arrived early. I pulled the curtains open, hung lights and sold concessions.

In tenth grade at Middletown High School in Rhode Island my French teacher, Jill Warren, the first person to look at me and see the potential for a future other than what my upbringing indicated, declared me a theatre director. I'm not sure exactly what she saw in me, but the particular way she looked at me made an enormous difference to the way I saw myself. She introduced me to art, film, music and ideas. She also directed plays for the school and I became her assistant. It was her idea to stage Eugene Ionesco's *The Bald Soprano* in the lunchroom that served as a theatre. Middletown High School's usual fare never stretched to anything as adventurous as this play from the French Absurdist movement. Ten days before opening, Mrs Warren caught the flu and asked me to take over the production. I did. And it was a success. I sometimes wonder if it were not a success, would I have had the courage to choose the theatre as a profession? But, largely due to her intervention, at the age of fifteen I decided definitively to become a director. In my senior year of high school I applied to Vassar College, Sarah Lawrence and several other good women's schools but was turned down by all of them. I ended up attending four colleges before I attained an undergraduate degree. I graduated in 1974 from Bard College where I directed many shows and joined a theatre company called Via Theater.

Via Theater, inaugurated by a fellow student, Ossian Cameron, was dedicated to a practical investigation into the work of Jerzy Grotowski. We remained together for two years, spent our school years executing physically gruelling work in a basement, and one summer toured the United States and Canada in a van: seven of us and a dog named Godot. Upon graduation from Bard College, Via Theater was invited to perform in Delhi, India, but the company dissolved with finality in Tel Aviv, Israel, en route to India. All of a sudden and for the first time in my life, I had no obligations. I was free and I could choose to go anywhere in the world. I knew instantly that New York City was the place I wanted to be.

I moved to New York City with a backpack and the 2000 dollars that remained from the money I had saved and earned for the trip to India. It was December of 1974. I found a loft on Grand Street in Soho – three bedrooms, a living room, a dining room, a dance studio and no heat. The entire rent was only 325 dollars a month which was not unusual in those heady early days of the Soho scene. I quickly found friends to share this loft and so each of us paid not much more than 100 dollars a person per month. During the following five years I held many jobs: I worked the phones in the collections department of a water company, I was an expense analyst in a brokerage firm on Wall Street, I watched over children in an afterschool theatre programme, I led workshops in a halfway house for mentally disabled people and I completed a masters degree in theatre history from the department at New York University now known as Performance Studies. I also directed lots of shows with actors who didn't mind working for no money in non-traditional spaces. I worked site specifically because I could not find a theatre in New York willing to take a chance on a young, untested director. I staged productions in shop windows, rooftops, construction sites, basements, a Romanian meeting hall, discos, clubs, a detective agency, an abandoned schoolhouse and many other places ripe for invasion.

Because of my unconventional theatre work, I was invited in 1979 to teach at the Experimental Theater Wing (ETW) which was, at that time, a relatively new and innovative undergraduate programme at New York University. ETW afforded me the time and facilities to grow as a director by originating new shows with students. The job also provided money to live on and enough to cover expenses for the other downtown theatre work I continued producing. It was at ETW that I met choreographer Mary Overlie, the inventor of the Six Viewpoints which I found to be an astonishing way of thinking about time and space. Her insights led me in the development of a new approach to training for actors.

It was around this time that I first encountered the work of the Schaubühne from Berlin. This adventure started when I saw a German film entitled *Sommergäste* based on Maxim Gorky's pre-revolutionary play *Summerfolk*. I sat in the cinema afterwards, paralysed with excitement and awe. I had never encountered the combination of such remarkable acting, beautiful imagery, political engagement and sheer intelligence. I was enraptured, moved and interested in *who* had created this work.

From the final film credits, I could discern that a German director, Peter Stein, and his theatre company, the Schaubühne, had filmed the play in West Berlin. Armed only with that information and a genuine interest to find out more, I signed up for German classes at the Goethe Institute in order to somehow get closer to these artists. The German language soon led me to a glossy and informative monthly German theatre magazine entitled *Theater Heute*. Each issue included information about theatre productions at the Schaubühne and described the plays and the processes of this unique theatre collective. I pored over the articles and photographs and started to incorporate their innovations into my directing.

Armed with this new input and stimulus, I continued directing shows in the context of the downtown New York low/no-budget arena, incorporating what I had learned. I engaged political issues in the context of every production. I experimented with new approaches to acting that changed my understanding of the actor's creative role in the realization of new productions and I experimented more consciously than ever with site-specific ideas.

I also began to receive phone calls from actors, writers and directors travelling from Germany who wanted to check out the theatre scene in New York City. Invariably they had been encouraged to call me by my colleagues who knew of my fascination with things German. These visitors stopped by my rehearsals and performances and I spent many late nights in East Village restaurants asking them every question I could think of about how they worked, what they had done and seen in Germany and what they thought about the art of the theatre. Occasionally I invited German actors to play roles in my plays in New York. Finally, *Theater Heute*, the source of my pilfering, published a sizable article about my work describing it as exemplary of the new American theatre scene. The great irony was that I had stolen so much from their own pages.

The article about my work in *Theater Heute* led to invitations to direct in Germany, Austria and Switzerland. I accepted everything and began a series of adventures in Europe that ultimately led me back to America with a deeper sense of myself as an American and a commitment to an investigation of American culture.

For the first job, directing a production with graduating students at the acting academy in West Berlin, I resolved to speak only German and to try to work like a German director. I did not like or trust my American background any more. I was sure that Americans were superficial and I wanted more than anything to be European. Determined to find a new way to be and work, I initiated a project with the students about the then hot topic of house-squatting in Berlin. The results were disastrous. In the process, I caught the German disease called *Angst*. I was afraid to set anything in rehearsal because I assumed that my every thought was superficial and that anything I could propose to the actors would be too facile. The production turned out to be a mess. With no solid form for the actors to push against and no rigour in thought or action, it was vague and confusing. German audiences filled the theatre every night to see the inferior work of the American director. They yelled at the stage, letting the actors know how bad it was. And it was bad.

It was in a pension in the Dolomite mountains in northern Italy after the Berlin failure that I had a big personal revelation that saved me. I realized with profound conclusiveness that I was an American; I had an American sense of humour, an American sense of structure, rhythm and logic. I thought like an American. I moved like an American. And, all at once, it was clear to me that the rich American tradition of history and people exists to tap into and own. Suddenly I was free. All the rest of my work in Europe and, in fact, since that moment in the pension in Italy, has been lighter and more joyful. I accepted and started to celebrate the shoulders upon which I stand.

This insight triggered an adventure in the theatre which continues for me to this day: an exploration of American culture. A great part of my work is American work, that is, it is about American historical events like vaudeville, marathon dancing and silent film as well as about certain American artists such as Gertrude Stein, Orson Welles, Emma Goldman, Andy Warhol, Robert Rauschenberg, or Robert Wilson, as well as musicals and plays by quint-essential American writers like William Inge, Elmer Rice, Leonard Bernstein, George S. Kaufman, etc. I'm interested in remembering and celebrating the American spirit in all of its difficult, ambiguous, and distorted glory.

It was Ariane Mnouchkine, the Artistic Director of Le Théâtre du Soleil in France, who directed me definitively towards the necessity of a company. When I asked her why she worked only with her company, she looked sternly at me and said, 'Well, you cannot do anything without a company. Don't get me wrong, companies are difficult. People leave and break your heart and the hardships are constant, but what are you going to accomplish without a company?' Her question induced a personal epiphany in which I realized that every great performance in theatre and dance I had ever experienced, without exception, was accomplished by a company.

Armed with this new understanding and a new necessity, I began to concentrate on creating the circumstances in which a company might be possible. I started by articulating my dream out loud, whenever possible, by describing what it was I imagined. When anyone asked me what I wanted, what I believed in, I invariably answered, 'A company'.

In 1989, when I became the second Artistic Director ever of Trinity Repertory Company in Providence, Rhode Island,

I inherited a substantial company of actors. It lasted one glorious, terrible year before the Board of Directors of the theatre found a way to force my departure. What I did learn is that you cannot take over someone else's company. You have to start from scratch.

The opportunity to start from scratch happened soon afterwards with the help and support of Japanese director Tadashi Suzuki. Not long after the Trinity débâcle, I was invited to Toga Mura, Japan, to participate in and observe the Toga International Arts Festival. Toga was Suzuki's summer residence in the green mountains far above the city of Toyama. Every year he invited artists and companies from around the world to perform at his festival. Suzuki and I hit it off and six months later in New York City, Suzuki, with the encouragement of Theatre Communications Group's director, Peter Zeisler, asked if I wanted to initiate a new enterprise with him. He proposed that together we would create a centre in the United States, not unlike his situation at Toga Mura, to advance the fellowship of theatre artists from around the world. 'You choose the place,' Suzuki said, 'because in five years I will have other things to do. I will help you get it started'. What he helped get started became my company, the SITI Company, which has been the centre of my creative work for the past ten years.

I chose Saratoga Springs, New York, as the place where Suzuki and I would establish our new venture. Saratoga is a beautiful town at the foot of the Adirondack Mountains, cultured yet quiet and only three hours from New York City. During the first several years of SITI's existence, the company travelled each summer to Toga Mura to work with both Suzuki and me on new productions which we would perform in Japan at the Toga Festival and then bring back to Saratoga. Suzuki and I gathered a group of American actors who became the core of the SITI Company. Each actor had to have trained in Suzuki's highly physical approach to acting so that they could perform in productions that he directed. They also trained in the Viewpoints with me.

The two disparate approaches to actor training produced a great alchemy. With no premeditated design or plan to put the two trainings together, it turned out that they served to counterbalance one another and the result was fortunate. Quite different in approach and derivation, the Suzuki method and the Viewpoints became the heart of the SITI Company's training and teaching. Introducing these two training methods into the same body results in strength, focus, flexibility, visibility, audibility, spontaneity and presence.

Although the SITI Company began as a summer operation, hosted by Skidmore College in Saratoga, it quickly grew into a year-round affair based in New York City. The company of actors, designers, technicians and managers who make up the SITI Company became my artistic family. Together we rehearse new shows, tour, teach, and every June conduct a month-long training programme in Saratoga for theatre artists from around the world. Although Suzuki did indeed withdraw from the company in order to go on to other projects, he has remained generous and supportive.

The SITI Company is now a group of very strong and wilful artists and friends who have created their own identity and signature. Sometimes it is frustrating to me that I get credit for what they, in fact, do. We put our heads together and push. The nature of our collaboration is expansive.

The members of the acting company are all, by nature, survivors who have developed a great respect for one another over time. They can speak frankly to each other about difficult things. All of them not only act in and tour new productions, but they teach Suzuki, Viewpoints and Composition everywhere we go. I owe Ellen Lauren, Will Bond, Tom Nelis, Akiko Aizawa, J. Ed Araiza, Barney O'Hanlon, Kelly Maurer, Jefferson Mays, Stephen Webber, and Leon Ingulsrud deep gratitude for their patience, perseverance and talent.

The design and technical team all have their own world-class careers but they come back to SITI to make work with the company as a way of flexing their muscles. Sound designer, Darron L. West, is the best dramaturge I've ever encountered. He is in rehearsal from day one and his sound-scapes are like an actor on the stage. Set designer, Neil Patel, constructs elegant arenas the actors use as a springboard. Mimi Jordan Sherin throws obstacles of light on to the stage for the development of every show. James Scheutte looks, listens and thinks, and then emerges with imaginative clothes that accentuate the space in which they appear.

As I write these words, the SITI Company is at the centre of my life. The journey leading up to the creation of this company is the journey of preparation to have a company. Ariane Mnouchkine was absolutely right: the condition of a company is a constant crisis. But it is a worthwhile crisis and an ongoing adventure.

Where the blips and bleeps lead now I do not know. And the story will always depend on who is reading it. But personally, I do know that I owe a great debt to the people who encouraged and inspired me. I am grateful for the ride.

memory ONE

(Virginia Woolf)

Inside every good play lives a question. A great play asks big questions that endure through time. We enact plays in order to remember relevant questions; we remember these questions in our bodies and the perceptions take place in real time and space. For example, the issue of *hubris* is an issue that humanity is still working on, which is why certain ancient Greek plays feel completely fresh and current. When I reach for a play on the shelf, I know that inside the book is a spore: a sleeping question waiting for my attention. Reading the play, I touch the question with my own sensibilities. I know that it has touched me when the question responds and provokes thought and personal associations – when it haunts me. Presently, everything I experience in daily life is in *relation* to it. The question has been unleashed upon my unconscious. In my sleep my dreams are imbued with the question. The disease of the question spreads out: to actors, designers, technicians and ultimately to the audience. In rehearsal we try to find shapes and forms to contain the living questions, in the present, on the stage. The act of remembering connects us with the past and alters time. We are living conduits of human memory.

The act of memory is a physical act and lies at the heart of the art of the theatre. If the theatre were a verb, it would be 'to remember'.

During the mid-1980s, the late Polish theatre director and philosopher Jerzy Grotowski accepted a position in the theatre department at the University of California at Irvine. The university agreed to build a studio to his specifications and to bring participants from around the world to work with him on what he called 'objective drama'. My friend, the actor Wendy Vanden Heuvel, travelled from New York to Irvine to participate in Grotowski's research and upon her return I asked about her experience. 'It was very frustrating at first,' she said. Asked to work intensively from sun-*down* until sun-*up*, she and participants from Africa, Southeast Asia, Eastern Europe, South America and the Middle East persevered for many weeks. Wendy's initial frustration stemmed from her trouble locating a source of energy and physicality to get through the long hours. After extreme physical exhaustion, the other participants would access familiar patterns and codes from their respective indigenous backgrounds. This seemed to give them an endless reservoir of energy as they began to dance and move in ways that were unique to their particular cultures, in ancient modes deeply imbedded in their corporeal memories. But for Wendy, nothing happened. As an American, she could find no deeply ingrained cultural resources that would help her to get through the endless nights. After a great deal of frustration and fatigue, and much to her relief, at last she touched upon her *Jewish* roots and from that source she unearthed familiar codes of sound and movement deeply rooted in the Jewish culture. Her body *remembered*.

Wendy's story worried me because I am not Jewish. Confronted with the same sleepless nights and physical exhaustion, how would *I* have moved? What are my codes? What would my body *remember*? I was also intrigued. What is culture? Where does theatre in the United States come from? Upon whose shoulders are we standing? What informs my artistic sensibilities? What is the role of memory?

I decided to conduct a roots search to find my place in the continuum of the history of the American theatre. I wanted to actively remember the past in order to use it. Whom and what could I channel? I wanted to feel the past and its people in the rehearsal room with me and allow them to influence my choices as a director. I started by attempting to identify dominant influences on my work.

The most immediate influences were easily accessible. During the late 1960s, theatre in the United States under-went an eruption, almost a revolution. I moved to New York City in 1974 and the atmosphere was still vertiginous. This cultural insurrection and its practitioners were a rich source of ideas and passion: the Living Theater, the Open Theater, the Manhattan Theater Project, the Performance Group, the Bread and Puppet Theater, the dancers at the Judson Church and individuals such as Robert Wilson, Richard Foreman and Meredith Monk. These artists felt almost present in my rehearsals. I was inspired and encouraged by their example and by their methods. They were the shoulders upon which I stood.

But it was the search beyond these immediate influences that became problematic. Much to my surprise and frustration, I discovered a serious blockage of information from earlier years. I could trace influences back to about 1968 and then everything stopped. I had difficulty channelling previous generations in any concrete way. I could not feel them 'in the room' with me. I wasn't using them in my rehearsals. I was not fed by them ideologically, technically, aesthetically or personally in a way that felt substantive or practical.

Certainly I was familiar with the prominent individuals and great companies from the first half of the century. I was aware of the political engagement and aesthetic breakthroughs of the Federal Theater Project, the Mercury Theater, the Group Theater, the Civic Theater, the Living Newspaper and individuals such as Eva Le Gallienne, Josh Logan, Hallie Flannagan, Orson Welles, Jose Ferrer, Elia Kazan, Clifford Odets and so many others, but why did I have so much trouble accessing their wisdom? Why could I not use and own their manifest political engagement and passionate relationship to social issues that so clearly influenced how they worked and what they accomplished? Other than the stale influence of a watered-down version of the Stanislavsky system, why could I not feel these people in the room with me? I felt cut off from their passion and commitment. I found it impossible to stand upon their values and ideals. Why could I not stand securely upon their shoulders? What happened?

I quickly ascertained that between the years 1949 and 1952, the theatre community in the United States was struck by a cataclysmic event: the McCarthy era. This political attack forced everyone to radically alter or adjust their lives and values. Some fled the country never to return, some were blacklisted and forced to stop working, and others just changed, recanted, disengaged and shut up. Today we barely remember the McCarthy era and most of us are not aware of the serious consequences of that forgotten catalyst. Through a brutally effective mechanism, artists were directed to disengage from issues facing the real world. Without this social link, many turned inward. What many of us don't realize is that this insipid political action has completely influenced the way we make work today. Like the consequences of Stalinism, the most effective political manoeuvre is one that is later forgotten. And we have forgotten because the actions of the McCarthy machine succeeded.

Born in 1951, I grew up with the notion that 'art and politics don't mix'. Now I had to ask myself, where did that maxim come from? Today we are largely oblivious to the repercussions of those dark years and unaware of the radical changes undergone by the people who were most effected by them. Their passionate commitment to the world around them and the kind of theatre that was born out of that passion is what I wanted to learn from and use. But we missed out. The manipulations of the House Committee on Un-American Activities generally wiped out lifelines to following generations.

Artists, suddenly absolved from any personal responsibility to the world around them, altered their ways and means. Painters embraced Abstract Expressionism, a movement which glorifies personal expression removed from any outside context and appropriately born directly upon the heels of McCarthyism. Everybody looked inward. Playwrights bore the brunt of the new charge to avoid political engagement. Plays became increasingly about 'you, me, our apartment and our problems'. The scope kept narrowing.

Fortunately, big-spirited playwrights like Suzan-Lori Parks, Chuck Mee, Anna Deâvere Smith, Emily Mann and Tony Kushner have begun to reverse the trend with plays that do re-engage big social issues. Examples are *America Plays*, *Investigation of a Murder in El Salvador*, *Fires in the Mirror*, *Execution of Justice* and *Angels in America*. These plays are renewed attempts to reconnect with social issues. As evidenced by the success of Kushner's play on Broadway, an appetite abounds for socially relevant work. I would like to suggest that this reconnection with the world is an act of life. Herbert Muschamp, reviewing a book on the Bauhaus in *The New York Times*, wrote:

● ● ● Artists should not distance themselves from their times. They
should leap into the fray and see what good they can accomplish
there. Instead of keeping a safe distance from the smelly swamp
of worldly values, they should dive right in and stir things up . . .
Modern Apollos want to make it in the marketplace; an artist's
integrity stands to be strengthened, not compromised, by
reckoning with the social reality.

At the risk of vast over-generalization, Americans profess
a lack of history. We are, as Gore Vidal designates us, the
United States of Amnesia. And yet, we share an extraordinary history: rich, complex and productive. In an
attempt to reconnect with sources earlier than 1968, I started
to examine the genesis of the performing arts in the United
States. My directing became an attempt to remember and to
reconnect with an artistic heritage. I concentrated on plays
by seminal American authors and new works about the
history of such ultra-American phenomena as vaudeville,
silent-film acting, and marathon dancing. I pursued my
ancestors in order to be actively related to them.

⬭

● ● ● The Historical sense involves a perception, not only of the
pastness of the past, but of its presence; the historical sense
compels a man to write not merely with his own generation in his
bones, but with a feeling that the whole of the literature of Europe
from Homer and within it the whole of the literature of his
own country has a simultaneous existence and composes a

simultaneous order. This historical sense, which is a sense of the timeless as well as of the temporal and of the timeless and of the temporal together, is what makes a writer traditional. And it is at the same time what makes a writer most acutely conscious of his place in time, of his own contemporaneity.

(T. S. Eliot)

Memory plays a huge role in the artistic process. Every time you stage a play, you are embodying a memory. Human beings are stimulated to tell stories from the experience of remembering an incident or a person. The act of expressing what is remembered is actually, according to the philosopher Richard Rorty, an act of *re-description*. In re-describing something, new truths are created. Rorty suggests that there is no objective reality, no Platonic ideal. We create truths by describing, or re-describing, our beliefs and observations. Our task, and the task of every artist and scientist, is to re-describe our inherited assumptions and invented fictions in order to create new paradigms for the future.

●●● Truth cannot be out there – cannot exist independently of the human mind . . . The world is out there, but descriptions of the world are not. Only descriptions of the world can be true or false. The world on its own – unaided by the describing activities of human beings – cannot.

(Richard Rorty)

If the McCarthy era dictated that art should have no connection to social and political systems, what remains is narcissism; the cult of the individual, the arrogant culture of the self.

What is culture? I believe that culture is shared experience. And it is constantly shifting. Ideas, in fact, are among the most contagious aspects of human culture. Imagine a huge field on a cold winter night. Scattered around the field are blazing fires, each with a group of people huddled close to stay warm. The fires represent shared experience, or the culture, of each group gathered around each fire. Imagine that someone stands up and walks across the cold, dark, windy field towards a different group gathered around another fire. This act of strength represents cultural exchange. And this is how ideas scatter.

In our culture, which is rapidly spreading around the world, collective action is suspect. We have been discouraged to think that innovation can be a collaborative act. There has to be a star. Group effort is a sign of weakness. We revere the cowboy riding out alone across the prairie. We are brought up to make money and spend it on ourselves. People are considered successful if they get rich and appear on television. Commercial success is applauded.

I want something else. I looked for a connection to an earlier American culture in order to find an alternate route into the future.

The McCarthy era was not the genesis of American paranoia. The theatre in the United States was not born a commercial entity although it became, to a large extent, dependent upon its mercantile viability. Choices were made and adjustments followed. To remember the people and the events and to *re-describe* them is to use them, to climb up on their shoulders and shout out loud.

Our cultural inclinations were forged by historical, social and political events and by people who had the courage to stand up and make their way across the cold field, to make choices: Rosa Parks, who wouldn't sit at the back of the bus, the factory workers who went on strike, Lillian Hellman, Martin Luther King, artists and scientists who broke classical rules. Our culture is contrived from social interactions and by the adjustments we make to change. When translated into different contexts, they have a chameleon capacity to change meaning – sometimes only slightly, sometimes radically.

The genesis of theatre in the United States makes a fascinating story. In order to sketch the landscape of our contemporary theatre scene, I will attempt to 're-describe' the history of performing arts in the United States. I will outline some events and jump from era to era to show that the shoulders upon which we stand are complex and diverse, driven by contradictory impulses and complicated agendas.

I decided to start from the very beginning. Chaos theory suggests that all phenomena are complexly connected and intertwined. A butterfly bats its wings in Honolulu and eventually engenders a typhoon in Japan. I wondered if I could locate the Big Bang in the theatre in the United States, for then I might be able to follow the repercussions and see if our experience today is the result of the fluttering of a butterfly's wings several hundred years ago. I wanted to see if the macrocosm contained the microcosm of the start.

The first play ever produced in the colonies was *Ye Bare and Ye Cubb*. It was performed in Fowkes' Tavern, a pub on the eastern shore of Virginia in 1665. After the initial performance, someone accused the play of blasphemy. The case was taken to court but the judge complained that he couldn't pass judgement on a play he hadn't seen. Therefore, the second performance of *Ye Bare and Ye Cubb* was performed in court! Afterwards, the judge ruled that the play was not blasphemous on the grounds that it was *entertaining*.

Is this event in 1665 a microcosm of the macrocosm of what the American theatre became? Is entertainment the bedrock of American theatre and the basis upon which all judgement of theatre originates? If the European humanist tradition perceives art as reflection, do we know it mainly as diversion?

The hard-working/hard-playing men who carved out the frontier craved live entertainment, the sleazier the better. Yet a puritanical ambivalence prevailed by marked resistance to theatrical presentations. Plays were denounced as snares of the devil by anti-theatre literature with titles like 'The Theater, the High Road to Hell'. The pioneers of the American theatre had to carve their stage out of a wilderness of bigotry and prejudice.

Another notable aspect of the growth of American theatre is the tremendous difficulty of its genesis. Population was sparse and it was extremely difficult to get from one place to another. The rigours of daily living in the seventeenth and eighteenth centuries are almost beyond our twenty-first-century comprehension.

Until 1775, Virginia and Maryland were the only two colonies which did not have anti-theatre laws at one time or another. Theatre's progress was impeded not only by moral prejudice, but by a rigid belief among the middle classes that stage productions were frivolous and wasteful of precious time. Even music confronted fervent religious resistance. In 1778, with the Colonial forces fighting for life and liberty, the Federal Congress adopted a law prohibiting theatre in any form.

Despite this resistance, a tremendous diversity of entertainment appeared in pre-Civil War America. The variety of ethnicities settling the colonies accounts for the heterogeneity: wagon shows, magic-lantern presentations, panoramas, circuses, minstrel shows, show boats or 'floating theatres', wild-west shows, melodramas, and travelling Shakespeare companies. Following the Civil War, literally hundreds of companies toured *Uncle Tom's Cabin*.

A minstrel show was the first theatrical production *exported* from the United States. White men in blackface sang and danced parodies of slave plantation entertainment to the great amusement of the European theatre-goers. Vaudeville – the word stems from the French *voix de ville*, voice of the cities – managed to incorporate sketches from the diverse urban immigrant groups under a single roof. For the first time people from different ethnic neighbourhoods came together who, under other circumstances, couldn't understand one another's languages and customs. Vaudeville was a loud and lively environment where cultures got to know one another through entertaining sketches and dramas. This highly popular phenomenon prevailed between 1865 and 1930. The genesis of film was partially responsible for its demise.

Despite the American Revolution and subsequent political independence, Americans felt culturally dependent on England and Western Europe for most of the eighteenth and nineteenth centuries. Before the twentieth century, there were very few American playwrights of consequence. The turn of the century changed all that. A sudden avalanche of activity galvanized the arts. By the end of the First World War, industrial America began to be a superpower and theatre artists, excited by new ideas from Europe and greatly influenced by psychoanalysis, feminism, progressive and radical politics, Post-impressionism, Expressionism and Symbolism, started to forge a modern American theatre. This new theatre favoured a rejection of verisimilitude, which had been a nineteenth-century preoccupation with photography. The pre-eminent designer Robert Edmund Jones advocated Expressionism over Realism:

●●● Realism is something we practice when we aren't feeling very well. When we don't feel up to making the extra effort.

Expressionism, on the other hand, was concerned with the expression of the inner self, the subconscious and its tension with surface reality. American playwrights began to experiment to great effect with Expressionism which became, for a while, the dominant force in the American theatre. Eugene O'Neill prescribed, 'Reject the banality of surfaces!' Expressionism was

●●● An intensity of vision which tries to catch the throb of life, necessarily doing violence to external facts to lay bare internal facts.

In addition to the early work of Eugene O'Neill, the Expressionist movement included American playwrights Elmer Rice, Susan Glaspell, John Howard Lawson and Sophie Treadwell. These artists rejected Realism and embraced theatricality and the poetry of the subjective experience. They supported native playwrights and were proponents of an American theatre inspired by but not emulating the newest art revolutions in Europe. Robert Edmund Jones declared, 'Think of it! No more tasteful, well furnished rooms with one wall missing.' Their strain of Expressionism can still be felt much later in Tennessee Williams's *Camino Real*, Thornton Wilder's *Our Town* and Arthur Miller's *Death of a Salesman*.

The dance world too, for the first time, produced radical alternatives to the pre-eminent world of ballet: Ruth St. Denis, Ted Shawn, Agnes DeMille and Martha Graham created companies and performances that seemed to spring from the American soil.

Perhaps the 1920s were a reflection of what Americans do best under pressure: a celebration of intensity, magnification, energy and industry; an ability to walk into the room bravely without knowing who or what is there. No other era comes close to the inconceivable outpouring of magnificent music and vigour onstage: George S. Kaufman and his collaborators, Jelly Roll Morton, Bessie Smith, Louis Armstrong, Ma Rainey, the Gershwins, Cole Porter, Ethel Merman, Billy Rose, Irving Berlin, George M. Cohan, Jerome Kern, Fanny Brice, Bert Williams, Oscar Hammerstein II and a whole lot more. In one year, 1926, Rodgers and Hart had five shows running or opening on Broadway. In 1927 Broadway reached its all-time production peak as critics from the twenty-four city daily newspapers grappled with 268 offerings.

The end of the 1920s brought the Depression. Vaudeville, the crown jewel of American popular entertainment, died as talking pictures replaced the art of the silent film. The talent drain into film started to dilute the potency of the stage. A new method for actors based on the early theories of the Russian Konstantin Stanislavsky came to dominate our approach to acting for the rest of this century.

Stanislavsky and his company, the Moscow Art Theatre, performed plays by Chekhov and Gorky in the United States during 1923 and 1924. By the time they got to America, these productions were already almost twenty years old and only reflected Stanislavsky's very early experiments in 'memory of emotion' and 'inner concentration'. But to American sensibilities, this revolutionary approach to acting had a tremendous impact on young theatre people, including Lee Strasberg, Stella Adler, Robert Lewis, Harold Clurman and many others who had never seen anything like this extraordinary acting company from Russia.

MEMORY

Greatly influenced by Pavlov's theories of conditioned reflexes and certain discoveries in the enticing, new frontier of the unconscious, Stanislavsky had developed methods of actor training that resulted in an arresting psychological realism and a remarkable acting ensemble able to portray human behaviour ultra-realistically. When Stanislavsky left America, Russian acting teachers connected to Stanislavksy's early research, including Richard Boleslavsky and Maria Ouspenskaya who remained in New York, were besieged to teach these methods to the ravenously enthusiastic young Americans. Lee Strasberg, who had himself been strongly influenced by the recent and fashionable ideas of Sigmund Freud, married his understanding of Stanislavsky with his passion for Freud and came up with powerful approaches to emotion and the unconscious using what we now know as affective memory, emotional recall and sense memory. This approach to acting became the Bible for the Group Theater, the Actors Studio, the Neighborhood Playhouse and many offshoots.

The Americans embraced the Russian experiments passionately and misguidedly by overemphasizing personalized emotional circumstances. Stanislavsky's system, now watered down to a 'method', proved effective for film and television, but in the theatre created an unfortunate stranglehold of emotional indulgence. I believe that the great tragedy of the American stage is the actor who assumes, thanks to our gross misunderstanding of Stanislavsky, 'If I feel it, the audience will feel it'.

The techniques derived from the Moscow Art Theatre's visit to America were, in fact, a narrow aspect of Stanislavsky's lifetime of work in the theatre. He quickly abandoned his early experiments in affective recollection and went on to make groundbreaking work in opera and to conduct experiments in physical action and something he called the psycho-physical unity of experience. Late in life, he rejected his earlier psychological techniques, calling them 'misguided'. But it was too late. Americans had already grabbed on to a severely limited aspect of his 'system' and turned it into a religion. The Americanization, or miniaturization, of the Stanislavsky system has become the air we breathe and, like the air we breathe, we are rarely aware of its omnipresence.

Where would we be now if the Moscow Art Theatre had *not* visited our shores? Would the Expressionist movement of the teens and twenties have developed into something even more exciting; would it have inspired more Expressionist masterpieces than *Camino Real*, *Our Town* and *Death of a Salesman*? Who and what would have been the great influences on the theatre? What about Martha Graham? Was she on to something that might have had a substantially more profound impact on the art of the theatre?

Martha Graham was becoming a major force during the 1920s. Like artists in the other fields, she was influenced by the same ideas that created Expressionism. I look to her now for inspiration and guidance.

Although she taught with Sanford Meisner at the Neighborhood Playhouse, Martha Graham's Expressionist approach to creating character has never really been translated for actors. For example, to create character in her dances, she would take the source and deconstruct the written text into a series of gestures that expressed the emotional life behind the words. According to her, a performer must search for the meanings behind gesture and expression and then reassemble them, working them into a pattern, a design, a purpose – into choreography. Martha Graham was a pioneer in our midst.

Today, much of our 'highbrow' mainstream theatre remains an imitation of the Western European tradition. Our native popular entertainments are considered 'lowbrow'. But this sense of inferiority and dependence belies the inherent difference between Europeans and Americans. Europeans are, generally speaking, a literary culture. Americans are an aural culture. Our dominant tradition is evangelical. For us, the *sound* of words takes precedent over their meaning. Although we pretend to be at ease with literature on stage like the Europeans are, in fact we are ill at ease. This pretence of ease makes for a false feel in the theatre.

In America we like to pretend that we have no history but, in fact, our history is rich and complex. I feel that we theatre practitioners today are too timid in our exploitation of the shoulders upon which we stand. Compared to the theatre's rapid growth and complex adjustments to the innovations, events and movements of the past several centuries, our progress now seems fainthearted. Acting, for example, is the only artistic enterprise in America that has not changed during the past three-quarters of a century. Most acting today looks pretty much the same as it did in the 1930s. Our work has not grown enough and our conventional goals seem too narrow.

I want an artistic explosion. Our present high-technology lifestyle demands a theatre experience that cannot be satisfied by video and movie screens. I want acting that is poetic and personal, intimate and colossal. I want to encourage the kind of humanity on the stage that demands attention and that expresses who we are and suggests that life is bigger. And it is for this reason that I'm trying to remember and study the past and combine it with the newest ideas in philosophy, science and art. In order to contribute to an artistic explosion I am researching new approaches to acting for the stage that combine vaudeville, operetta, Martha Graham and postmodern dance. I want to find resonant shapes for our present ambiguities. I want to contribute to a field that will engender moments on-stage that broaden the definitions of what it means to be human.

Theatre is *about* memory; it is an act of memory and description. There are plays and people and moments of history to revisit. Our cultural treasure trove is full to bursting. And the journeys will change us, make us better, bigger and more connected. We enjoy a rich, diverse and unique history and to celebrate it is to remember it. To remember it is to use it. To use it is to be true to who we are. A great deal of energy and imagination is demanded. And an *interest* in remembering and describing where we come from.

Robert Edmond Jones wrote this in *The Dramatic Imagination*:

●●● In all these dramas of the past there is a dream – an excitement, a high, rare mood, a conception of greatness. If we are to create in the theatre, we must bring back this mood, this excitement, this dream. The plain truth is that life has become so crowded, so hurried, so commonplace, so ordinary, that we have lost the artist's approach to art. Without this, we are nothing. With this, everything is possible. Here it is, in these old dramas. Let us see it. Let us learn it. Let us bring into the theatre a vision of what the theatre might be. There is no other way. Indeed, there is no other way.

If we can see ourselves in relation to our predecessors and the impulses behind their innovations, our own theatre will necessarily become more intense, poetic, metaphoric, humane and expressive. Our collective dreams will be bigger; the arenas will become more compelling. Perhaps as we remember the past we will find ourselves able to create with more energy and articulation.

⊂⊃

●●● If I can see far, it is because I stand on the shoulders of giants.

(Isaac Newton)

As a result of a partnership with memory and the consequent journeys through the past, I feel nourished, encouraged and energized. I feel more profoundly connected to and inspired by those who came before. I feel the courage to articulate for my profession because the shoulders upon which I'm standing feel sturdy. The journeys through the past inspired and encouraged me to develop new productions about Americans and our history. And these encounters with remarkable men and women have made me feel these people are my colleagues. The research led me to new ways of thinking about acting, playwrighting and design. And I recognized that there is such a thing as an American sense of structure, an American sense of humour, and a way of listening and responding that is culturally rooted. Confronted with sleepless nights and physical exhaustion, I might even find some ancestral ways to move.

Violence

● ● ● Concerning all acts of initiative and creation, there is one elementary truth, the ignorance of which kills ideas and splendid plans; that the moment one definitely commits oneself, the Providence moves too.

All sorts of things occur to help one that would never have occurred. A whole stream of events issues from the decision, raising in one's favor all manner of unforeseen incidents and meetings and material assistance, which no man could have dreamt would have come his way.

Whatever you can do, or dream you can, begin it. Boldness has genius, power and magic in it.

(Goethe)

Watching director Robert Wilson in rehearsal, I realized, for the very first time, the necessity for violence in the creative act. It was the spring of 1986, and up till this moment I had never had the opportunity to watch another director rehearse with actors.

The production was Heiner Müller's *Hamletmachine* performed by undergraduate acting students at New York University. The rehearsal was scheduled to begin at 7 p.m. I arrived early to find a buoyant atmosphere. In the back row of the theatre, PhD students and scholars waited expectantly, pens poised, for Wilson's entrance. On the stage young actors warmed up. A stage management team sat behind a battalion of long tables at the edge of the stage. Wilson arrived at 7.15. He sat down in the middle of the audience risers amidst the bustle and noise and proceeded to gaze intently at the stage. Gradually everyone in the theatre quietened down until the silence was penetrating. After about five excruciating minutes of utter stillness, Wilson stood up, walked towards a chair on the stage and stared at it. After what felt to me an eternity, he reached down, touched the chair and moved it less than an inch. As he stepped back to look at the chair again, I noticed that I was having trouble breathing. The tension in the room was palpable, almost unbearable. Next, Wilson motioned an actress towards him in order to show her what he wanted her to do. He demonstrated by sitting on the chair, tilting forward, and moving his fingers slightly. Then she took his place and precisely copied his tilt and hand gestures. I realized that I was leaning forward on my own chair, deeply distressed. Never having experienced another director at work, I felt like I was watching other people in a private, intimate act. And I recognized that night the necessary cruelty of decision.

The decisive act of setting an object at a precise angle on the stage, or an actor's hand gesture, seemed to me almost an act of violation. And I found this upsetting. And yet, deep down, I knew that this violent act is a necessary condition for all artists.

Art is violent. To be decisive is violent. Antonin Artaud defined cruelty as 'unrelenting decisiveness, diligence, strictness'. To place a chair at a particular angle on the stage destroys every other possible choice, every other option. When an actor achieves a spontaneous, intuitive, or passionate moment in rehearsal, the director utters the fateful words 'keep it', eliminating all other potential solutions. These two cruel words, 'keep it', plunge a knife into the heart of the actor who knows that the next attempt to re-create that result will be false, affected and lifeless. But, deep down, the actor also knows that improvisation is not yet art. Only when something has been decided can the work really begin. The decisiveness, the cruelty, which has extinguished the spontaneity of the moment, demands that the actor begin an extraordinary work: to resurrect the dead. The actor must now find a new, deeper spontaneity within this set form. And this, to me, is why actors are heroes. They accept this violence and work with it, bringing skill and imagination to the art of repetition.

It is significant that the French word for rehearsal is *repetition*. Certainly it can be argued that the art of the theatre is the art of repetition. (The English *rehearsal* proposes to re-hear. The German *Probe*, suggests an investigation. In Japanese, *keiko* translates to practice. And so on. A study of different languages' words for rehearsal is endlessly

45
●

fascinating.) In rehearsal an actor searches for shapes that can be repeated. Actors and directors together are constructing a framework that will allow for endlessly new currents of vital life-force, emotional vicissitudes and connection with other actors. I like to think of staging, or blocking, as a vehicle in which the actors can move and grow. Paradoxically, it is the restrictions, the precision, the exactitude, that allows for the possibility of freedom. The form becomes a container in which the actor can find endless variations and interpretive freedom.

For the actor, this necessary violence in creating a role for the theatre is distinctly different from the violence necessary in acting for the camera. In film acting, the actor can afford to do something impulsively without any concern for repeating it endlessly. What is vital for the camera is that the moment be spontaneous and photogenic. In the theatre it must be repeatable.

Great performances exude both exactness and a powerful sense of freedom. This freedom can only be found within certain chosen limitations. The limitations serve as a lens to focus and magnify the event for the audience as well as to give the actors something to measure themselves against. A limitation can be as simple as staying in the appropriate light and speaking the text exactly as written or as difficult as performing complex choreography while singing an aria. These limitations invite the actor to meet them, disturb them, transcend them. An audience experiences the actor testing his or her limits; expressing beyond the ordinary despite the limitations.

Early in his career, Chuck Close, the American photo-realist painter specializing in close-up portraits and self-portraits, decided that he wanted to be more than a technician. He began to set himself intense limitations in his manner of painting in order to transcend craftsmanship. He felt that these limitations, either structural or material, tested his creativity and magnified his achievements. The ultimate limitation occurred in 1988 when he suffered a stroke and was paralysed due to a blood clot in his spinal column. He regained partial use of his arms, and was able to return to painting after developing techniques which allowed him to work from a wheelchair. He was forced to relearn painting from his wheelchair with brushes tied to his hands. These strict limitations, quite beyond any he could dream up for himself, encouraged him to make a remarkable transition in his approach and resulted in what might be the most significant work of his lifetime.

To be articulate in the face of limitations is where the violence sets in. This act of necessary violence, which at first seems to limit freedom and close down options, in turn opens up many more options and asks for a deeper sense of freedom from the artist.

Yo Yo Ma, the virtuoso cellist, goes out of his way to work in musical arenas outside of his classical experience. He has made several recordings of Appalachian music with ace fiddler Mark O'Connor. In order to adapt his classical training to meet the demands of O'Connor and Appalachian music, Ma purposefully changed the way he held his bow. He positioned his hand at the bottom of the bow rather than the customary classical placement. Suddenly, the virtuoso cellist, Ma, felt totally out of his element with this new limitation. But eventually this unfamiliar way of playing opened up new possibilities and a new kind of eloquence.

●●● I ended up using a way of playing that Baroque players use. Baroque players have less of a need to fill large spaces. You have infinitely more opportunity to create another layer of rhythm. In fact, it changed how I play Bach now. You can actually develop a tremendous variety of inflection without losing rhythmic clarity.

Yo Yo Ma risked failure. Risk is a key ingredient in the act of violence and articulation. Without embracing the risk, there can be no progress and no adventure. To attempt to perform articulately from a state of imbalance and risk imbues the action with extraordinary energy.

We tremble before the violence of articulation. And yet, without the necessary violence, there is no fluent expression. When in doubt, I look for the courage, in that moment, to take a leap: articulate a thing, even if I'm not sure it is right or even appropriate. Armed with only a hunch, I try to take the plunge and in the midst of the plunge I strive to be as articulate as I can be. 'If you cannot say it,' wrote the philosopher Ludwig Wittgenstein, 'point to it.' In the midst of frightening uncertainty, I try to lean into the moment and point clearly. Even if I don't know at what angle a chair should be on the stage, I try to act decisively anyway. I do the best I can. I make decisions before I'm ready. It is the attempt to articulate that is both heroic and necessary.

One day, unable to attend rehearsal for the remount of a play I had directed with my company, the SITI Company, I invited one of my graduate directing students from Columbia University to cover for me. The next day I asked company member Ellen Lauren how the young man had performed as substitute director. 'Not very well,' she said. 'Why not?' I asked. 'Well, he didn't say anything.' She explained that, from her point of view, it doesn't really matter how erudite or naive the observation, but, as an actor, she needs the person responsible for watching, the director, to say *something* around which she can organize her next attempt. To try to say something in a state of flux even if you do not know the right thing to say is the point. Make an observation. To be silent, to avoid the violence of articulation alleviates the risk of failure but at the same time there is also no possibility of advancement.

> He either fears his fate too much
> Or his deserts are small
> Who dares not put it to the torch
> To win or lose it all.

I learned about the Japanese word *irimi* while studying Aikido, a Japanese martial art. Simply translated, *irimi* means, 'to enter' but it can also be translated 'choose death'. When attacked, you always have two options: to enter, *irimi*, or to go around, *ura*. Both, when accomplished in the right manner, are creative. To enter or 'to choose death' means to enter fully with the acceptance, if necessary, of death. The only way to win is to risk everything and be fully willing to die. If this is an extreme notion to occidental sensibilities, it does make sense in creative practice. To achieve the violence of decisiveness, one has to 'choose death' in the moment by acting fully and intuitively without pausing for reflection about whether it is the right decision or if it is going to provide the winning solution.

It is also valuable to know when to use *ura*, or going around. Patience and flexibility is an art. There is a time for *ura*, going around, and there is a time for *irimi*, entering. And these times can never be known in advance. You must sense the situation and act immediately. In the heat of creation, there is no time for reflection; there is only connection to what is happening. The analysis, the reflection and the criticism belong before and after, never during, the creative act.

As a young director I was better at *ura*, going around, than at *irimi*, entering. In rehearsal I felt timid about interrupting the actors at work. Afraid to be decisive about any specific blocking or staging, anxious that my intervention would destroy the fresh, spontaneous life that seemed to be happening so naturally without my contribution, I kept quiet. Then, of course, opening night approached and panic would ensue. Suddenly the lack of anything solid or tangible for the actors to push against was painfully obvious to me. 'What have we been doing all this time?' I would ask myself in the light of no agreements, no staging, no trampoline with which the actors might tempt the heights. Suddenly, forced by pressure and circumstance, I would spring into high gear and negotiate with the actors to find moments, actions and patterns to repeat and depend upon. Finally these agreements became the springboards for the actors which would allow them to meet one another with assurance and stability and would, at the same time, encourage them to take the essential risks and intuitive leaps within the framework of the actions and words. After a while, I found the necessary courage to make these agreements earlier and earlier in the rehearsal process. I learned how to enter.

Athol Fugard, the South African playwright, described censorship as hesitation. For him censorship is not necessarily the proximity of government inspectors or a threat of imprisonment but, rather, on the physical hesitation of his hand while writing. Censorship is his own private vacillation provoked by whatever doubts are out to ambush him. Censorship is a physical hesitation in the light of a fleeting thought or doubt about how his peers might receive what he is writing, whether or not they will like it or if it will get published. In the light of our hesitations, we must be deeply connected to the act. We must be decisive and intuitive simultaneously.

Richard Foreman, perhaps the most intellectual of American directors, said that, for him, creation is one hundred per cent intuitive. I have learned that he is right. This is not to say that one must not think analytically, theoretically, practically and critically. There is a time and a place for this kind of left-brain activity, but not in the heat of discovery in rehearsal and not in front of an audience. As soon as the door closes in rehearsal or as soon as the curtain goes up in performance, there is no time to think or reflect. In these moments of exquisite pressure there is only the intuitive act of articulation within the crisis of action. No more than a painter can pause in the moment of interaction with paint and canvas should a rehearsal process get bogged down in theory. I think of a good rehearsal as being like the experience of playing the Ouija board. You place your hands on the pulse and listen. You feel. You follow. You act in the moment before the analysis, not after. This is the only way.

⬭

Distortion is a partial destruction and it is a necessary ingredient in making the vague visible. It too is violent. Agnes DeMille described the use of distortion, or turning, in dance:

●●● Distortion is the very essence of art and all dancing. Distortion is what saves ordinary rhythmic movement from being bland paddling in the air. Distortion is the extension of effort, the prolongation or stress beyond the norm. It can be arresting or remarkable, and it can help fix the gesture in memory – yes, and in meaning, because it spells difficulty overcome, human dominance, and triumph.

To be awake on the stage, to distort something – a movement, a gesture, a word, a sentence – requires an act of necessary violence: the violence of undefining. Undefining means removing the comfortable assumptions about an object, a person, words, sentences or narrative by putting it all back in question. What is instantly definable is often instantly forgettable. Anything onstage can be asleep when it is overly defined.

Victor Schklovsky, the Russian Formalist who undoubtedly influenced Bertolt Brecht with his *Four Essays on Formalism* written in the 1920s, developed significant theories on the function of art. Everything around us, he wrote, is asleep. The function of art is to awaken what is asleep. How do you awaken what is asleep? According to Schklovsky, you turn it slightly until it awakens.

Bertolt Brecht, probably influenced by Schklovsky's writings, developed theories about making the strange familiar and the familiar strange in the articulation of the alienation (*Verfremdung*) effect. He must have used the notion of turning something, distorting it making it unfamiliar, until it awakens in order to see it anew in his approach to acting for the stage.

An example of this Schklovsky-ian notion of distortion or 'turning' can be found in Alfred Hitchcock's film *Suspicion*. In one sequence, a husband (Cary Grant) climbs a staircase carrying a glass of milk on a tray to his wife (Ingrid Bergman) who lies ill in bed in a room at the top of the stairs. At this particular moment, the suspense lies in wondering whether or not the husband has poisoned the milk. Is he a loving husband or a villain and an assassin? What is not obvious but certainly affects the way we experience the scene, is the quality of the milk. Hitchcock placed a tiny light bulb, invisible to the audience, into the glass of milk so that it would glow just a little. Although the audience is not sure why, the milk seems somehow alive, awake, undismissible and in a state of dangerous potential.

⊂⊃

●●● Creativity is first of all an act of destruction.

(Pablo Picasso)

Violence for a painter is the very first brush stroke on a canvas. Everything after that in the work on the painting, as Picasso indicated, is about correcting that initial action.

●●● When you begin a picture, you often make some pretty discoveries. You must be on guard against these. Destroy the thing, do it several times. In each destroying of a beautiful discovery, the artist does not really suppress it, but rather transforms it, condenses it, makes it more substantial. What comes out in the end is the result of the discarded finds. Otherwise, you become your own connoisseur. I sell myself nothing.

(Pablo Picasso)

An audience in the theatre should be engaged by the events but also slightly distressed about what is happening. The interactions, the words and the actions onstage have to be fresh and untamed and undismissible. Actors are confronted with the enormous task of awakening sleeping clichés. For example, the words 'I love you', because they have been said so often, have no meaning unless they are undefined, distorted, turned and offered up anew. Only then might they be fresh and hearable. Picking up a teacup has been done so many times that it is often defined and categorized before the action has begun. When an action is defined by the actor before it is executed, the action will be asleep. It will not 'glow'. An artist enters into a relationship with the materials at hand in order to wake them, untame them. To release the potential in a word or action requires the actor to perform in such a way that does not describe its meaning but rather turns it slightly so that the multiplicity of its potential meanings are evident and awake.

●●● If a phenomenon can be defined as 'it is that, and only that,' that means it exists only in our heads. But if it has a real life existence, we can never hope to define it completely. Its frontiers are always moving, while exceptions and analogies keep opening up.

(Jerzy Grotowski)

○

Another kind of violence is the violence of disagreement. I believe that it is in disagreement that certain truths about the human condition are revealed. It is when images, ideas or people disagree that one senses the truth. These disagreements can be found everywhere in art.

Towards the end of Bernardo Bertolucci's film *Last Tango in Paris*, two lovers, played by Marlon Brando and Maria Schneider, sit at a small table in a tango palace. Schneider, in close-up, brutally informs Brando, with whom she has shared an intense sexual relationship, that she is finished with him. She declares that she's going to get up and leave him there and insists that she doesn't ever want to see him again. As she speaks, the camera pans back and you see that she is also jerking him off under the table. In that moment, the audience is confronted with two polar opposites: attraction and desire for escape. Within these two opposites lies the untamed and complex truth about being alive.

Truth, which is an *experience* and not something easily defined, mostly exists in the space between opposites. It exists in the disagreement of ideas or imagery. In the example from *Last Tango in Paris*, the truth about that complex relationship could not exist in the space of one idea. It is expressed in the tension between opposites, the opposition of physical attraction and desire for escape. Opposition, or dialectic, sets up alternative systems of perceiving. It creates shock spaces where insight might occur.

In the film of the musical *Cabaret* is a scene in which a handsome blonde boy stands up in a beer garden in pre-war Germany and sings 'Tomorrow Belongs to Me'. It is a beautiful, sunny day and, one by one, other people in the garden stand with him and sing along. After a while, the blonde boy lifts his arm, upon which is affixed a swastika.

At that moment, the modern-day audience is confronted with two extremes: (1) the song is catchy, the boy is attractive, and if you had been there that day, you might have joined in prior to the revelation of the swastika, and (2) a knowledge of the historical consequences of Nazism. These two opposing associations set up an *experience*, not an answer. Truth is in the tension between opposites.

One cannot look directly at the truly big human issues any more than one can look directly at the sun. In order to see the sun you look slightly to the side. Between the sun and where you are looking is the perception of the sun. In art and in the theatre we use metaphor as the thing to the side. Through metaphor we see the truth about our condition. The word metaphor comes from the Greek *meta* (above) and *pherein* (to carry). Metaphor is that which is carried above the literalness of life. Art is metaphor and metaphor is transformation.

⬭

Violence begins with decision, with commitment to something. The word commit derives from Latin, *committere*, which means 'to ignite action, to bring together, join, entrust, and *do*'. Committing to a choice feels violent. It is the sensation of leaping off a high diving-board. It feels violent because the decision is an aggression against nature and inertia. Even as seemingly small a choice as deciding the precise angle of a chair feels like a violation of the free flux and flow of life.

But most artists would agree that their work does not proceed from an idea of what the finished product will be; rather it emerges out of a passionate excitement about the subject matter.

●●● The poet's poem is wrung from him by the subject which excites him.

(Samuel Alexander)

To generate the indispensable excitement there must be something at stake, at risk, something momentous and uncertain. A sure thing does not arouse us emotionally.

There is no disgrace in not knowing what you are doing and not having all the answers. But your passion and excitement about something will take you the distance through uncertainty. If you are insecure and do not really know what you are doing, it's fine. Just try to work with an interest in exactitude. Be exact with what you do not know. Realism on the stage is generated, not by a general feeling for reality or truth, but, rather, it emerges in the act of exactitude and decisiveness with something that excites you.

While I was the Artistic Director of Trinity Repertory Theatre in Providence, Rhode Island, a young under-graduate directing student at Brown University invited me to watch a run-through of her production. When I arrived in the rehearsal hall she indicated that it would take a few minutes before the cast was ready to begin. Naturally she was nervous about the run-through and about me being there. I sat down to wait and watched the young director make a fatal flaw. An actor approached her and asked what he should do with a particular chair. In her haste and nervousness, she said these words: 'It doesn't matter.'

Something matters to an audience only if you make it matter. If you attend to it, if only for a moment, the commitment of your attention will create the tension of attention. If something is not attended to decisively by the actor and the director, then it will not be attended to by the audience. It will be invisible. The act of decision gives presence to the subject. The young director could have taken just an instant to commit her attention to the problem. She could have turned the actor's question around and asked him where he thought the chair might go. She might have looked puzzled for a moment and then, from her real state of insecurity, been decisive.

⬭

Robert Wilson's rehearsal of *Hamletmachine* brought home to me the legitimacy and necessity of violence in the creative act. To decide is an act of violence, yet decisiveness and cruelty are part of the collaborative process that the theatre offers. Decisions give birth to limitations which in turn ask for a creative use of the imagination.

I work with a company, the SITI Company, because it is a group of artists who have learned to disagree with one another with generosity. We developed a way to use violence with compassion and kindness. I find this approach essential to my way of working. To be cruel is ultimately an act of generosity in the collaborative process. 'Ideas are cheap' we always say in the heat of a rehearsal. Ideas come and go but what is important is the commitment to a choice and to its clarity and communicativeness. It's not about the right idea or even the right decision, rather it is about the quality of decisiveness. We try to work intuitively with one another, our collective hands on the Ouija board, and then, in the right moment, we enter. We 'choose death'.

eroticism

 THREE

●●● There is a tension that goes all the way through a piece of music and never lets up. A long silver cord that one pulls on. Sometimes there's a little kink in the cord, but it never sags. There's always a force irresistibly pulling it from the first note to the last. You've got to get the audience from the first note.

(Alfred Brendel)

The role of attraction and eroticism in the theatre is rarely discussed and yet both are vital ingredients in the creative act and in the dynamics between audiences and the actors. In order to investigate the issues of attraction and eroticism, this chapter follows the archetypal pattern of a passionate relationship.

1 Something or someone stops you in your tracks.
2 You feel 'drawn' to it.
3 You sense its energy and power.

4 It disorientates you.

5 You make first contact; it responds.

6 You experience extended intercourse.

7 You are changed irrevocably.

1 Something or someone stops you in your tracks

Not long ago while visiting the Museum of Modern Art in San Francisco, I encountered a gigantic painting by Anselm Kiefer entitled *Osiris and Isis*. My plans to visit the entire museum that day were sabotaged. I could not get past this one intense, attractive, vibrant, disturbing, undismissable canvas. I was confronted with the magnitude of its ideas, shapes, violence, movement and the endless vistas that opened up while encountering this work. Stopped in my tracks, I could not walk past it and go on to other paintings. I had to meet it, deal with it. It challenged me and it changed me.

What stops us in our tracks? I am rarely stopped by something or someone I can instantly know. In fact, I have always been attracted to the challenge of getting to know what I cannot instantly categorize or dismiss, whether an actor's presence, a painting, a piece of music, or a personal relationship. It is the journey towards the object of attraction that interests me. We stand in relation to one another. We long for the relationships that will change our vistas. Attraction is an invitation to an evanescent journey, to a new way of experiencing life or perceiving reality.

An authentic work of art embodies intense energy. It demands response. You can either avoid it, shut it out, or meet it and tussle. It contains attractive and complicated energy fields and a logic all its own. It does not create desire or movement in the receiver, rather it engenders what James Joyce labelled 'aesthetic arrest'. You are stopped in your tracks. You cannot easily walk by it and go on with your life. You find yourself in *relation* to something that you cannot readily dismiss.

In *A Portrait of the Artist as a Young Man*, James Joyce differentiates *static* and *kinetic* art. He values static art and disparages kinetic art. I find his conception of static and kinetic challenging and helpful in thinking about what we put on the stage. Kinetic art moves you. Static art stops you. Pornography, for example, is kinetic – it can arouse you sexually. Advertising is kinetic art – it can induce you to buy. Political art is kinetic – it can move you to political action. Static art, on the other hand, stops you. It causes arrest. Much like the painting by Anselm Keefer, it won't let you easily walk by it. Static art offers a self-contained universe unified only in its complex, contradictory fields. It does not remind you of anything else. It does not create desire in you and it does not move you in an easy manner. You are stopped in your tracks by its unique power. When confronted with Cézanne's great paintings of apples, for example, you do not desire to eat the apples. You are, rather, confronted by the appleness of the apples! The apples stop you in your tracks.

With *Osiris and Isis*, I was stopped by the magnitude of this particular painting's inner drama. It invited me to engage with it. I was called to the adventure of a relationship.

In the first stage of a relationship, something or someone stops us in our tracks. Something is asked of us; a response is requested. The more valuable the potential relationship, the less able we are to dismiss the invitation.

The great experiences I have enjoyed in the theatre have always asked a lot of me. Sometimes I fear that I'm being asked more than I feel ready to give. But the 'call to adventure' is unmistakable. I am invited on a journey. I am called upon to respond with the fullness of my being.

In the theatre, the way a show begins has everything to do with the quality of the journey. Do the first moments stop me in my tracks? And how do they do that? As an audience, I can usually feel the promise of a remarkable theatre experience in the very first instants. How does it begin? What expectations are engendered initially, and then are those expectations fulfilled or broken? The best beginnings feel both surprising and inevitable. Perhaps it starts too abruptly, or it seems too quiet or loud or too fast or slow, but the way a production begins should already question the familiar range and my habitual perceptions. If I am lucky, I am stopped in my tracks.

A good actor stops me in my tracks too. The quality of their stillness or movement or speaking is hard to dismiss. Although I am not aware of what it is that they are doing to generate this magnetic presence, I know that I cannot look away. I cannot walk on.

What is the actor doing to stop me in my tracks? She or he sets up a complex inner landscape and attempts to remain present within it. The actor simultaneously actualizes the many languages of the stage, including time, space, text, action, character and story. The accomplishment is an extraordinary feat of juggling many things at once. The act of speaking becomes dramatic because of the change that occurs inside the person who is present, in the moment, engaged in speech. And I, too, am present there, in relationship to this person juggling.

2 You feel 'drawn' to it

We are each incomplete. We are drawn towards the other in search of completeness. We sense the potential closing of a circle. And this sensation, this potential, lies at the very heart of what draws us to the theatre.

The Oxford English Dictionary defines attraction as (1) 'the action of a body in drawing another towards itself by some physical force such as gravity, magnetism'. (2) 'The action of causing people or animals to come nearer by influencing their conscious actions, providing favourable conditions'. (3) 'The action or capacity of eliciting interest, affection, sympathy'. (4) 'Drawing forth a response'. Also, 'A force acting mutually between particles of matter, tending to draw them together, and resisting their separation'.

I once met a man aboard a ship on the Mediterranean. We were both leaning against the railing watching the water pile up below us. He told me about his life's work and his great interest in the essential human attraction to dramatic intersections of the natural elements. He suggested that human beings are attracted, physically and emotionally, towards places where the elements meet: where earth meets water, and water meets air, and air meets fire, etc.

I have experienced the sensation of being drawn towards the edge of a cliff to experience the sea battering up below, or towards a clearing in the woods where I might glimpse a mountain against the sky. It is a deeply intrinsic physical attraction that moves me towards the places where the elements meet.

In art and in theatre I am also drawn to the places where the elements meet. I crave an arena that embraces the exquisite tension of opposing and attracting forces. An encounter with a painting like *Osiris and Isis*, or being in the proximity of an exciting actor engaged in the act of juggling time and space simultaneously, ignites in me an attraction that is undeniable. I am drawn towards them, not in their familiarity, but in their unfamiliarity.

A theatre critic once suggested that the American fear of art is actually a puritanical fear of the sexual encounter. But erotic tension between the stage and the beholder is part of what makes the theatre experience so attractive. The theatre is a place where it is possible to meet one another in an energetic space unmediated by technology. The sensory stimulation allowed in theatre, authorized by its very form, allows the corporeal imagination to exercise itself.

Eroticism is excitation, sensory excitation, caused by human sensual stimuli. Erotic tension between actors and audience is part of the recipe for effective drama. The attraction of the theatre is the promise of a proximity with actors in a place where the corporeal imagination might experience extended intercourse.

Erotic tension between actors happens more than anyone can imagine. In the exquisite pressure of time and space, actors are caught up in a very human drama – the drama of co-presence. In rehearsal and in front of the public, this co-presence, this space between actors, must necessarily be charged.

Erotic tension between a director and an actor can be an indispensable contribution to a good rehearsal process. As a director, I do not encourage physical consummation of this erotic tension, but I do believe that the tension is an important ingredient in the recipe for engaging theatre. En route to rehearsal I want the sensation of heading towards an exciting, romantic, turbulent rendezvous. A rehearsal should feel like a date. Both as a director and as an audience member, I want to find the actors attractive, uncategorizable and undismissable. The best productions I have directed issue from a rehearsal process charged with erotic interest.

3 You sense its energy and power

●●● The art of performance depends on the relationship between the musician and the audience. In the concert hall, each motionless listener is part of the performance. The concentration of the player charges the electric tension in the auditorium and returns to him magnified . . . The audience grows together and becomes a

group. There's the impression of a journey undertaken together
and a goal achieved.

(Alfred Brendel)

A great actor, like a great striptease artist, withholds more
than she or he shows. Artists, as they mature, come closer
to the great wisdom found in the potent combination of
physical containment and emotional expansion. Restraint
is key. Take the moment and all of its complexities; concentrate it, let it cook, and then contain it. This concentration
and restraint generates energy in the actor and interest in
the audience. Zeami, the Japanese originator of Noh drama,
suggested that the actor should always withhold a certain
percentage of her or his passion.

●●● When you feel ten in your heart, express seven . . .

An actor's special gift is the ability to resist, to hold back, to
tame, to keep energy in, to concentrate. With this compression, the actor plays with the spectators' kinesthetic
sensibilities and prevents them from predicting what is
about to happen. In every moment, the aim is to conceal
the predetermined structure and the outcome from the
spectator.

This ability to stimulate the audience to crave, to
experience desire rather than sating it, is part of the
actor's art. I always feel that the best actors possess a secret
that they enjoy keeping from me. The spectator should
be drawn to the stage like a detective hot on the trail of

a crime. The actor chooses when to hide and when to reveal.

As I sit in an audience during a play, I am always acutely, sometimes painfully, aware of the creative tension or the lack of tension between actors and audience. The theatre is what happens between spectator and actor. The dynamics between an actor and the audience constitutes a creative relationship that is at once intimate and distanced and which is very different from daily life. The relationship is circular. The actor is completely dependent upon the creative potential of each audience member and must be able to adjust and respond to whatever ensues. The actor initiates and the audience completes the circle with their imagination, memory and creative sensibilities. Without a receiver, there is no experience.

When I go to the theatre, I want to sense the energy and power of the event. And I want to be considered part of the act. I want to be in a relationship. And I want something to happen.

4 It disorientates you

Art, like life, is understood through experience, not explanations. As theatre artists, we cannot create an experience for an audience; rather, our job is to set up the circumstances in which an experience might occur. Artists are always dependent upon the person at the receiving end of their work. The South African playwright Athol Fugard said that he writes with hope because of the person at the other end of his writing. We issue an invitation. We hope that we have left enough clues so that the audience will pick up the trail where we leave off.

Every great journey begins with disorientation. Children naturally spin one another blindfolded before an adventure. Alice falls down a rabbit-hole and changes size or travels through a looking-glass to enter her wonderland. We all, audience and artists alike, have to allow for a little personal disorientation to pave the way for experience.

I am afraid of falling. I spent years studying the Japanese martial art Aikido because of the amount of time one must spend upside down in the training. I try to welcome the disorientation as a necessary practice for my work in rehearsal. I know that I must learn to welcome disorientation and imbalance. I know that the attempt to find balance from an imbalanced state is always productive and interesting and yields rich results. I try to welcome the disorientation in order to allow for real love.

Falling in love is disorientating because the boundaries between new lovers are not fixed. In order to fall in love, we have to let go of our daily habits. In order to be touched, we have to be willing not to know what the touch is going to feel like. A great theatre event is also disorientating because the boundaries between who is giving and who is receiving are not distinct. An exciting artist plays with our expectations and with our memory. This interchange allows for the living interactive art experience.

●●● There is no limit to the horizon, and no 'method', no experiment, even of the wildest – is forbidden, but only falsity and pretence. 'The proper stuff of fiction' does not exist; everything is the proper stuff of fiction, every feeling, every thought; every quality of brain and spirit is drawn upon; no perception comes amiss.

(Virginia Woolf)

I want to use the theatre to question the limits and boundaries of human experience. In every play I direct I want to question my formal, aesthetic, structural and narrative assumptions. I want to allow for necessary personal disorientation in order to make contact with the material and the people involved. And I want to include disorientation as a thread in the fabric of every production.

5 You make first contact; it responds

The virtuoso pianist Alfred Brendel, in an interview for the *New Yorker*, described the role of the audience in his concerts.

●●● The public sometimes thinks an artist is a television set – something comes out, nothing goes back. They don't realize that if they can hear me, then I can hear them – their coughs, the electronic beeps from their wristwatches, the squeaking of their shoes.

A performance has fluid rhythm that changes with each audience it touches. An actor can feel an audience as palpably as the audience can feel the actors. The late Ron Vawter, an actor with the Wooster Group, told me that he could feel the intelligence of an audience and he found it distressing that European audiences are far more intelligent than American audiences.

Quantum physics teaches us that the act of observation alters the thing observed. To observe is to disturb. 'To observe' is not a passive verb. As a director I have learned that the quality of my observation and attention can determine the outcome of a process. Under the right circumstances the audience's observation and attention can significantly affect the quality of an actor's performance. Actors can respond to an audience's powers of observation. It is the contact/response cycle at the heart of live performance that makes being there so extraordinary.

●●● One doesn't stop learning. I've learned how to control certain silences. They depend not just on what you play, but on how you look. After the last chord of Opus 111, I don't move, I don't take my hands away from the keyboard, because directly I stir they applaud. Each time I play the Beethoven cycle, the silence gets longer, because I know how to relate to it, I know how to sit still.

(Alfred Brendel)

Several years ago I returned to Cambridge, Massachusetts to attend the final performance of my production of Kaufman and Hart's *Once in a Lifetime* at the American Repertory Theater. I asked Christine Estabrook, the actress playing the comedic role of the gossip columnist, how the performances had been received by the audiences. 'Oh,' she answered, 'there have been good audiences and bad audiences.' 'What do you mean?' I asked. 'Well, some of our audiences have had bad timing. Some laugh too long and some laugh just the right amount of time.'

After opening night, once the director, the playwright and the designers have gone away, the actor is left with a very particular daily dilemma: the quality of the relationship between the stage and the seats. The actor stands backstage and listens to the audience before making an entrance. The reception is palpable. Listening to the listening, the actor makes adjustments in the speed of an entrance, the intensity of the first line spoken or the length of a pause. An actor learns when to hold back and when to open up based on the agility of the audience.

Occasionally, in preparation for a concert, Alfred Brendel invited his neighbour and friend A. Alvarez to his home in London to listen to him play the piano. The first time Alvarez accepted the invitation, he worried that Brendel expected criticism or feedback, but soon he understood the invitation. Alvarez would arrive in Brendel's home to find a chair sitting next to the piano. 'What I assume,' writes Alvarez, 'is that he wants a sympathetic and attentive presence in the room, simply to complete the artistic circle.'

The audience is engaged in a collaboration of silence which makes possible the extended intercourse of performance.

6 You experience extended intercourse

Attention is a tension. Attention is a tension between an object and the observer or a tension between people. It is a listening. Attention is a tension over time.

As a director, my biggest contribution to a production, and the only real gift I can offer to an actor, is my attention. What counts most is the quality of my attention. From what part of myself am I attending? Am I attending with desire for success, or am I attending with interest in the present moment? Am I hopeful for the best in an actor or do I want to prove my superiority? A good actor can instantly discern the quality of my attention, my interest. There is a sensitive life-line between us. If this line is compromised, the actor feels it. If it is cheapened by my own ego or desire or lack of patience, the line between us is degraded.

A South African actress described a bad rehearsal with a director whose quality of attention was compromised. She looked up from the stage during a difficult scene to find the director riding an exercise bicycle *and* eating popcorn while he watched her work.

The image of this man on his exercise bike is disturbing to me because a director's primary task is the opposite of narcissism. A director's job is to be connected to the stage, physically, imaginatively and emotionally. The director tries to be the best possible audience. The late William Ball, the founding Artistic Director of ACT/San Francisco, wrote in his book *A Sense of Direction* that he considers an audience heroic because they choose to spend two hours not thinking about themselves. A director should attend to an actor as the most discriminate and attentive audience member.

The quality attention one offers in rehearsal is the key to a fertile process. The rehearsal is a microcosm of the extended intercourse of attention offered by an audience. It is a place of potential rapture. In a rehearsal room, like making love, the outside world is excluded. It is a process of arousal, heightened sensation, alive nerve endings and sudden pinnacles. It is an extreme event separate from our daily lives and it is a place to meet one another.

A production is also only that possibility. It is a time set aside from daily life in which something might occur. We issue invitations to a party where there is the potential for extended intercourse.

7 You are changed irrevocably

A passionate relationship transpires when the quality of attention to it reaches a boiling point. The eroticism is created by the tension of attention and the attention is generated by interest. And interest is not something that can be faked. Not really.

All the journeys that have transpired in my life have been animated by interest. Something or someone has stopped me in my tracks. Interest, that thing that cannot really be faked, is an invitation to adventure. It has always been disorientating to do, but I have had to act on these interests. Somehow I know that in order to keep on working as an artist, I have to keep on changing. And this means that when interest is piqued, I must follow or die. And I know that I will have to hang on tight for the ride. These rides have changed me irrevocably.

The primary tool in a creative process is interest. To be true to one's interest, to pursue it successfully, one's body is the best barometer. The heart races. The pulse soars. Interest can be your guide. It always points you in the right direction. It defines the quality, energy and content of your work. You cannot feign or fake interest or choose to be interested in something because it is prescribed. It is never prescribed. It is discovered. When you sense this quickening you must act immediately. You must follow that interest and hold on tight.

At the moments when interest is piqued, when you find yourself stopped in your tracks, you will find yourself instantaneously at a crossroad. At this crossroad the definitions and assumptions that shaped and guided you to the present moment disintegrate; all that remains is a feeling of disorientation, an unbridled excitement, a sensation of being drawn out, an *interest*.

If the interest is genuine and large enough and if it is pursued with tenacity and generosity, the boomerang effect is resounding. Interest returns volley to affect your life and inevitably alter it. You must be available and attentive to the doors that open unexpectedly. You cannot wait. The doors close fast. It will change your life. It will give you adventures you never expected. You must be true to it and it will be true to you.

The interest lives in between us and the object of our interest. In this moment we live in-between. We travel outward to make contact with the other. The word interest is derived from the Latin *interesse* which is the combination of *inter* (between) and *esse* (to be): to be between. The state of interest is a liminal experience – the sensation of a threshold. Interest is personal and temporal. It changes, it vacillates and should be attended to in every moment because it is a guide.

Interest is my guide in choosing a play to direct and it is my guide through rehearsal. I try to be aware, at any particular moment, of what I am really interested in. It is a light sensitivity and yet is my connection to the process. Sometimes what I am interested in has not been planned and yet, despite the possible disruption, I must follow it.

The interest in someone or something always engenders response and the ensuing intercourse of interaction can change us for ever. Great plays endure through time because they address critical human issues that are still vital to a culture. When we reach out to a play, when we make contact, we create a relationship with those issues. Interest is our guide. Interest arouses attention. Attention arouses the object of our attention. We interact with interest and attention to these themes and they respond. And in this interaction, something happens that changes us. Our task is to find forms in which the interaction might inhabit the present moment. Our hope is that it will be perceivable to others who will be stopped in their tracks, sensing its energy and power.

terror

FOUR

> ●●● A large part of our excessive, unnecessary manifestations come
> from a terror that if we are not somehow signaling all the time
> that we exist, we will in fact no longer be there.
>
> (Peter Brook)

My first encounters with theatre were startling and exposed me to art alive with an unnameable mystery and danger. These early experiences have made it difficult for me to relate to art that is not rooted in some form of terror. The energy of individuals who face and incorporate their own terror is genuine, palpable and contagious. In combination with the artist's deep sense of play, terror makes for compelling theatre both in the creative process and in the experience of an audience.

I grew up in a Navy family and we moved every year or two to a new naval base in another part of the country or another part of the world. My cultural references were

Disney movies, cocktail parties, and aircraft carriers. My first brush with terror in art happened in a park in Tokyo, Japan, when I was six years old. A huge white painted face leered down at me from an immense multicoloured body. I hid, terrified, behind my mother's skirt. This horrendous and beautiful vision was my first exposure to an actor in costume wearing a mask. A few months later, in the same city, I watched, terrified, as huge wooden altars borne high by drunken Japanese men charged down the streets of Tokyo on a holy day. The drunken men and the altars sporadically smashed into shopwindows. The men seemed out of control, out of their minds and utterly unforgettable.

At fifteen, when my father was stationed in Newport, Rhode Island, I saw my first professional theatre production at Trinity Repertory Company, in Providence, Rhode Island. The National Endowment for the Arts (NEA) had granted the company enough money to bring every high school student in the state into the theatre to see their plays. I was one of those students and travelled to Providence in a big yellow school bus to see Shakespeare's *Macbeth*. The production terrified, disorientated and bewildered me. I couldn't figure out my orientation to the action. The witches dropped unexpectedly out of the ceiling, the action surrounded us on big runways and I didn't understand the words. The unfamiliar English sounded like a foreign language and the fantastic visual language, also strange to me, made my first encounter with Shakespeare extraordinary. This production of *Macbeth* constituted my first encounter with the disorientating poetic language of the stage where size and scale could be altered by the artist to create unforgettable journeys for the audience. The experience was frightening but compelling. I didn't *understand* the play, but I knew instantly that I would spend my life in pursuit of this remarkable universe. On that day in 1967, I received my first lesson as a director: *never talk down to an audience*. It was immediately clear to me that the experience of theatre was not about us understanding the meaning of the play or the significance of the staging. We were invited into a unique world, an arena that changed everything previously defined. The Trinity Company could have easily used their big grant to present facile children's theatre and fulfil their requirements to the NEA. Instead, they presented a complex, highly personal vision in a compelling, rough fashion. The production and the artists involved spoke to me directly in a visceral and fantastic manner.

Most of the truly remarkable experiences I've had in the theatre have filled me with uncertainty and disorientation. I may suddenly not recognize a building that was once familiar or I cannot tell up from down, close from far, big from little. Actors I thought that I knew are entirely un-recognizable. I often don't know if I hate or love what I am experiencing. I notice that I am sitting forward, not leaning back. These milestone productions are often long and difficult; I feel disjointed and a little out of my element. And yet I am somehow changed when the journey is completed.

We are born in terror and trembling. In the face of our terror before the uncontrollable chaos of the universe, we label as much as we can with language in the hope that once

*high stakes = terror

we have named something we need no longer fear it. This labelling enables us to feel safer but also kills the mystery in what has been labelled, removing the life and danger from what has been defined. The artist's responsibility is to bring the potential, the mystery and terror, the trembling, back. James Baldwin wrote, 'The purpose of art is to lay bare the questions which have been hidden by the answers.' The artist attempts to undefine, to present the moment, the word, the gesture as new and full of uncontrolled potential.

I became a theatre director knowing unconsciously that I was going to have to use my own terror in my life as an artist. I had to learn to work in trust and not in fear of that terror. I was relieved to find that the theatre is a useful place to concentrate that energy. Out of the almost uncontrollable chaos of life, I could create a place of beauty and a sense of community. In the most terrible depths of doubt and difficulty, I found encouragement and inspiration in collaborating with others. We have been able to create an atmosphere of grace, intensity and love. I have created a refuge for myself, for actors and for audiences through the metaphor that is theatre.

I believe that theatre's function is to remind us of the big human issues to remind us of our terror and our humanity. In our quotidian lives, we live in constant repetitions of habitual patterns. Many of us sleep through our lives. Art should offer experiences that alter these patterns, awaken what is asleep, and remind us of our original terror. Humans first created theatre in response to the everyday terror of life. From cave drawings to ecstatic dances around numberless fires; from Hedda Gabler raising her pistol, to the disintegration of Blanche Dubois, we create shapes that deal with our distress. I have found that theatre that does not channel terror has no energy. We create out of fear, not from a place of security and safety. According to the physicist Werner Heisenberg, artists and scientists share a common approach. They enter into their work with one hand firmly grasping the specific and the other hand on the unknown. We must trust ourselves to enter this abyss with openness, with trust in ourselves, despite the unbalance and vulnerability. How do we trust ourselves, our collaborators and our abilities enough to work within the terror we experience in the moment of entering?

In an interview with *The New York Times*, one actor, William Hurt, said, 'Those who function out of fear, seek security, those who function out of trust, seek freedom.' These two possible agendas dramatically influence the creative process. The atmosphere in the rehearsal hall, therefore, can be imbued with either fear or trust. Are the choices made in rehearsal based on a desire for security or a search for freedom? I am convinced that the most dynamic and thrilling choices are made when there is a trust in the process, in the artists and in the material. The saving grace in one's work is love, trust and a sense of humour – trust in collaborators and the creative act in rehearsal, love for the art and a sense of humour about the impossible task. These are the elements that bring grace into a rehearsal situation and onto the stage. In the face of terror, beauty is created and hence, grace.

I want to create theatre that is full of terror, beauty, love and belief in the innate human potential for change. Delmore Schwarz said, 'In dreams begin responsibility.' How can I begin to work with this spirit and this responsibility? How can I endeavour not to conquer but to embrace terror, disorientation and difficulty?

Every time I begin work on a new production I feel as though I am out of my league; that I know nothing and have no notion how to begin and I'm sure that someone else should be doing my job, someone assured, who knows what to do, someone who is really a professional. I feel unbalanced, uncomfortable and out of place. I feel like a sham. In short, I am terrified.

Normally, I find a way to make it through the research and table-work stage of rehearsal, where the necessary dramaturgical discussions, analysis and readings happen. But then, always, the dreaded moment arrives when it is time to put something on to the stage. How can anything be right, true or appropriate? I desperately try to find an excuse to do anything else, to procrastinate further. When we do finally have to begin work on the stage, everything feels artificial, arbitrary and affected to me. And I am convinced that the actors think that I am out of my mind. Every time the dramaturge steps into the rehearsal hall, I am sure that they are distressed that nothing we are doing reflects the previous dramaturgical discussions. I feel unsophisticated and superficial. Fortunately, after a while in this dance of insecurity, I start to notice that the actors are actually beginning to transform the senseless staging into something I can get enthused about and respond to.

I have spoken with a number of theatre directors and found that I am not alone in this sensation of being out of my league at the beginning of rehearsals. We all tremble in terror before the impossibility of beginning. It is important to remember that a director's work, as with any artist, is intuitive. Many young directors make the big mistake of assuming that directing is about being in control, telling others what to do, having ideas and getting what you ask for. I do not believe that these abilities are the qualities that make a good director or exciting theatre. Directing is about feeling, about being in the room with other people; with actors, with designers with an audience. It is about having a feel for time and space, about breathing, and responding fully to the situation at hand, being able to plunge and encourage a plunge into the unknown at the right moment. David Salle, the painter, said in an interview:

●●● I feel that the only thing that really matters in art and life is to go against the tidal wave of literalism and literal-mindedness to insist on and *live* the life of the imagination. A painting has to be the experience instead of pointing to it. I want to have and give *access to feeling*. That is the riskiest and only important way to connect art to the world – to make it alive. The rest is just current events.

I know that I cannot sit down when work is happening on the stage. If I sit, a deadness sets in. I direct from impulses in my body responding to the stage, the actors' bodies, their inclinations. If I sit down I lose my spontaneity, my connection to myself, to the stage and to the actors. I try to soften my eyes, that is, not to look too hard or with too much desire, because vision is dominant and eviscerates the other senses.

When I am lost in rehearsal, when I am stymied and have no idea what to do next or how to solve a problem, I know that this is the moment to make a leap. Because directing is intuitive, it involves walking with trembling and terror into the unknown. Right there, in that moment, in that rehearsal, I have to say, 'I know!' and start walking towards the stage. During the crisis of the walk, something *must* happen; some insight, some idea. The sensation of this walk to the stage, to the actors, feels like falling into a treacherous abyss. The walk creates a crisis in which innovation must happen, invention must transpire. I create the crisis in rehearsal to get out of my own way. I create despite myself and my limitations, my private terror and my hesitancy. In unbalance and falling lie the potential to create. When things start to fall apart in rehearsal, the possibility of creation exists. What we have planned before, our dramaturgical decisions, what we have previously decided to do, in that moment is not interesting or productive. Rollo May wrote that all artists and scientists, when they are doing their best work, feel as though they are not doing the creating; they feel as though they are being spoken through. This suggests that the constant problem we face in our rehearsals is *how do we get out of our own way*? How can we become a vessel through which we are spoken? I believe that part of the answer is the acceptance of terror as primal motivation and then a full body-listening to what develops out of it.

For me, the essential aspect of a given work is its vitality. This vitality, or energy, is a reflection of the artist's courage-ousness in the face of her or his own terror. The creation of art is not an escape from life but a penetration into it. I saw a retrospective of Martha Graham's early dance works before the company's unfortunate demise. I was astonished that pieces such as *Primitive Mysteries*, which are now over fifty years old, were *still* risky and exposed. Graham once wrote to Agnes DeMille:

●●● There is a vitality, a life-force, a quickening that is translated through you into action, and because there is only one of you in all time, this expression is unique. And if you block it, it will never exist through any other medium and be lost. The world will not have it. It is not your business to determine how good it is; nor how valuable it is; nor how it compares with other expressions. It is your business to keep it yours clearly and directly, to keep the channel open. You do not have to believe in yourself or your work. You have to keep open and aware directly to the urges that motivate you.

Vitality in art is a result of articulation, energy and differ-entiation. All great art is differentiated art. Our awareness of the differences between things around us touches upon the source of our terror. It is more comfortable to feel similarities; yet we have to accept the terror of differences in order to create vital art. The terrible truth is that no two people are

87
●

alike, no two snowflakes are alike, no two moments are alike. Quantum physicists say that nothing touches, nothing in the universe has contact; there is only movement and change. This is a terrifying notion given our attempt to make contact with one another. The ability to see, experience and articulate the differences between things is called *differentiation*. Great artworks are differentiated. An exceptional painting is one in which, for example, colours are highly and visibly differentiated from one another, in which we see the differences in textures, shapes, spatial relationships. What made Glen Gould a brilliant musician was his openness to high differentiation in music, which created the ecstatic intensity of his playing. In the best theatre, moments are highly differentiated. An actor's craft lies in the differentiation of one moment from the next. A great actor appears dangerous, unpredictable, full of life and differentiation.

We not only need to use our terror of differentiation but also our terror of conflict. Americans are plagued with the disease of agreement. In the theatre, we often presume that collaboration means agreement. I believe that too much agreement creates productions with no vitality, no dialectic, no truth. Unreflected agreement deadens the energy in a rehearsal. I do not believe that collaboration means mechanically doing what the director dictates. Without resistance there is no fire. The Germans have a useful word that has no suitable English equivalent: *Auseinandersetzung*. The word, literally 'to set oneself apart from another', is usually translated into English as 'argument', a word with generally negative connotations. As much as I would be happier with a congenial and easygoing environment in rehearsal, my best work emanates from *Auseinandersetzung* which means to me that to create we must set ourselves apart from others. This does not mean 'No, I don't like your approach, or your ideas.' It does not mean 'No, I won't do what you are asking me to do.' It means 'Yes, I will include your suggestion, but I will come at it from another angle and add these new notions.' It means that we attack one another, that we may collide; it means that we may argue, doubt each other, offer alternatives. It means that feisty doubt and a lively atmosphere will exist between us. It means that I will probably feel foolish and unprepared as a result. It means that rather than blindly fulfilling instructions, we examine choices in the heat of rehearsal, through repetition and trial and error. I have found that German theatre artists tend to work with too much *Auseinandersetzung*, which becomes debilitating and can create static, heady productions. Americans tend towards too much agreement, which can create superficial, unexamined, facile art.

These words are easier to write than to practise in rehearsal. In moments of confrontation with terror, disorientation and difficulty, most of us want to call it a night and go home. These thoughts are meant to be reflections and notions to help give us some perspective, to help us to work with more faith and courage. I'd like to close with a quote from Brian Swimme.

●●● How else can we express feelings but by entering deeply into them? How can we capture the mystery of anguish unless we become one with anguish? Shakespeare lived his life, stunned by its majesty, and in his writing attempted to seize what he felt, to capture this passion in symbolic form. Lured into the intensity of living, he re-presented this intensity in language. And why? Because beauty stunned him. Because the soul can not confine such feelings.

Stereotype

● ● ● The problem with clichés is not that they contain false ideas, but rather that they are superficial articulations of very good ones. They insulate us from expressing our real emotions. As Proust himself put it, we are all in the habit of 'giving to what we feel a form of expression which differs so much from, and which we nevertheless after a little time take to be reality itself'. This leads to the substitution of conventional feelings for real ones.

(Christopher Lehman-Haupt)

In this chapter, I examine our assumptions about the meaning and uses of stereotype, cliché and inherited cultural memory. I am interested in these issues both from the point of view of the artist's interaction with them and the audience's reception of them.

In conversation with the Japanese director Tadashi Suzuki in a living room in San Diego, I started to suspect my deeply ingrained assumptions about stereotypes and clichés. We were discussing actors and acting when he mentioned the dread word, 'stereotype'. Suzuki is renowned for his iconoclastic productions of Western classics done in a distinctly Japanese fashion. For many years he worked with the extraordinary world-class performer Kayoko Shiraishi. Some claim that she is the best actor in the world. With Suzuki, she created the central roles around which he built many landmark productions. In 1990 she left his company to pursue an independent career.

Through a translator, Suzuki intimated his chagrin that Shiraishi had been invited by Mark Lamos, then Artistic Director of Hartford Stage in Connecticut, to play Medea in a production at his theatre. Unhappy about the prospect of Shiraishi appearing in Lamos's production, Suzuki complained that the results would be unfortunate. At first I protested. What a wonderful idea for an actor of her skill and calibre to appear in a play at an American regional theatre. Suzuki still looked unhappy and I assumed a kind of *hubris* on his part; I thought that he was troubled by the notion of another director having a success with 'his' actor. Finally I began to understand that the reason was far more complex and fascinating.

Hartford audiences, Suzuki explained, would be charmed by Shiraishi's distinctly Japanese approach to acting because to them it would seem exotic. They would be enchanted with the Kabuki and Noh influences and by the remarkable way she spoke and moved. But, he continued, Lamos would not see the necessity of driving Shiraishi through these Japanese stereotypes towards genuine expression.

Audiences would be satisfied with the exoticism but would go home without the real goods.

Intrigued by Suzuki's mention of stereotype and by the dilemma that international exchange presents in the light of codified cultural behaviour, I wanted to pursue the subject.

In rehearsal, Suzuki went on, Shiraishi always started out as the weakest actor in the room. Everything she did was an unfocused cliché. While all the other actors managed to rehearse well, she would struggle crudely with the material. Eventually, 'fuelled by the fire he lit under her', as Suzuki described it, the clichés and stereotypes would transform into authentic, personal, expressive moments and finally, with the proper prodding, she would ignite and eclipse everyone around her with her brilliance and size.

The notion of putting a fire under a stereotype stopped me in my tracks. I started to wonder about the negative connotations around the word stereotype and about my persistent efforts to avoid them.

In my own rehearsals, I had always mistrusted clichés and stereotypes. I was afraid of settling on any solution that wasn't completely unique and original. I thought that the point of a rehearsal was to find the most inventive and novel staging possible. Suzuki's dilemma started me wondering about the meaning of the word stereotype and about how we handle the many cultural stereotypes we inherit. Should we assume that our task is to avoid them in the service of creating something brand-new, or do we embrace the stereotypes; push through them, put a fire under them until, in the heat of the interaction, they transform?

Perhaps stereotype might be considered an ally rather than an enemy. Perhaps the obsession with novelty and innovation is misguided. I decided to study this phenomenon and my assumptions around innovation and inherited tradition.

In his essay 'Tradition and the Individual Talent', T. S. Eliot suggests that an artist's work should be judged not by its novelty or newness, but rather by how the artist handles the tradition he or she inherits. Historically, he wrote, the concept of originality referred to the transformation of tradition through an interaction with it as opposed to the creation of something brand-new. More recently, the art world became obsessed with innovation.

Actually, the word stereotype stems from the Greek *stere*, solid or solid body; having or dealing with three dimensions of space. *Type* comes from the word pressure or pounding, such as the action of typing on a typewriter. In the original French, stereotypes were the first printing machines. A stereotype was a plate cast from a printing surface. The French verb *stereotype* means to print from stereotyped plates. The word cliché came from the sound of metal jumping when the ink dye is struck during the printing process.

The negative connotations first arose in the nineteenth century in England when stereotype began to refer to authenticity in art: 'The standardized figurative sense of an image, formula, or phrase cast in a rigid mould'. During the twentieth century, stereotype continued to accrue disparaging definitions: 'An oversimplified opinion, prejudiced attitude or uncritical judgement; a set of wide generalizations about the psychological characteristics of a group or class of people; a rigid, biased perception of an object, animal, individual or group; a uniform, inflexible mode of behaviour; a standardized mental picture that's held in common by members of a group; to reproduce or perpetuate in an unchanging or standardized form; cause to conform to a fixed or preconceived type'.

I like that the etymology of stereotype refers to solidity. These inherited solid shapes, images and even prejudices can be entered and embodied, remembered and reawoken. If we think of a stereotype as three-dimensional, as a container, isn't it encouraging to interact with substantial shapes in the hyper-ephemeral art of the theatre? Isn't 'putting a fire' under inherited stereotypes a very clear and specific action in a field which is so much about remembering? The task is suddenly so concrete, so definite. A stereotype is a container of memory. If these culturally transmuted containers are entered, heated up and awakened, perhaps we might, in the heat of the interaction, reaccess the original messages, meanings and histories they embody.

Perhaps we can stop trying so hard to be innovative and original; rather, our charge is to receive tradition and utilize the containers we inherit by filling them with our own wakefulness. The boundaries of these containers, their limits, can serve to magnify the experience of entering them.

Because we can walk and talk, we assume that we can act. But an actor actually has to reinvent walking and talking to be able to perform those actions effectively upon the stage. In fact, the most familiar actions are perhaps the most difficult to inhabit either with fresh life or a straight face. When asked to walk downstage carrying a gun while saying the words 'You've ruined my life for the last time', an actor senses the danger that all of these sounds and movements might be hackneyed and predictable. The concern is real and concrete. If the actor has preconceived assumptions about how to perform the actions and words, the event has no chance to come to life. The actor must 'put a fire' under these clichés in order to bring them to life.

In life and in representations of life, so much has been done before and said before that they have lost their original meanings and have been transmuted into stereotype. Representations of life are containers for meaning which embody the memory of all the other times they have been done.

In 1984 I directed a production of the Rodgers and Hammerstein musical *South Pacific* with undergraduate acting students at New York University. I wanted to channel the sizzling energy of the original 1949 production, so we set our show in a clinic for war-damaged young people who had undergone stressful experiences in the then-current political crises in Grenada and Beirut. The clinic was a fictional invention which offered a contemporary context in which the musical could be performed intact. Each actor played a 'client' whose therapy for their particular trauma was to play various roles in *South Pacific* as part of the graduation ceremony from the clinic.

The rehearsals began with an investigation of the under-lying sexual and racial tensions inherent in the musical. I asked the actors to create compositions around specific themes. At one rehearsal I asked the men and the women to divide into male/female pairs. Each couple was to compose seven physical 'snapshots' illustrating archetypical patterns found in male/female relationships. The women were to portray men and the men women. I asked the men to guide the women in selecting and portraying the male archetypes, and the women were each to show their male partners how to embody the archetypes of women. I never anticipated the ensuing fireworks. The energy in the room as the actors created the snapshots accelerated until I thought that the roof would lift off the studio. Because of the gender switch, the actors felt the freedom to enter and embody certain taboo stereotypes with pleasure, zeal and intimacy. The inter-action between the men and women was so intense that it affected our entire rehearsal process and galvanized the performances. Fire had been placed under the stereotypes of male/female behaviour.

Although sexual and behavioural stereotypes abounded in commercials, songs and movies, it was socially taboo during the 1980s for these young men and women to enact them. Exaggerated macho behaviour and stereotypical expressions of feminine acquiescence were politically incorrect and the issue was a particularly heated one because it was considered exploitive of women and insensitive to men. But in the context of the rehearsal where the roles were reversed, the permission to recreate the clichés, to put the fire under the stereotypes, released a volatile and priceless energy within the stereotypical snapshots. The staging became a container for released energy. The result was sexy, vital and powerful performances by the young actors. The stereotypes became meaningful because they were presented to the audience outside a commercial context. We were not trying to sell goods; rather, within the context of theatre, audiences and actors alike dealt in a fresh and critical way with the sexual stereotypes we live with daily.

⸺

It is natural to want to avoid stereotypes because they can be oppressive and dangerous to certain people. For example, racial stereotypes make fun of and degrade people in a way that is hurtful and insulting. Stereotypes *can* be oppressive if they are blindly accepted rather than challenged. They *can* be dangerous because without 'putting the fire under them', they will reduce rather than expand. They can be negative because historically people have been reduced to the bias of stereotype.

The decision to position a minstrel show at the very heart of my production *American Vaudeville* required that everyone involved in it confront history and stereotype in a very personal and immediate way. Performed by the entire cast of eighteen actors, the minstrel show was to be the centrepiece of our production.

American Vaudeville was one of a trilogy of plays I created about the roots of American popular entertainment. I wrote the play with Tina Landau and directed it at the Alley Theater in Houston, Texas, in 1991. A composite of rich American performance traditions, vaudeville flourished in the United States between 1870 and 1930. Within this populist entertainment empire, many cultures performed under the same roof with audiences from numerous immigrant backgrounds who gathered to enjoy the display of wit and spectacle. The acts, chock-full of stereotypes, were highly entertaining to a country of immigrants getting to know one another. Irish and German humour, family acts and minstrel shows were featured alongside Shakespeare, operatic renditions and new dance forms.

Handling ethnic stereotype in contemporary society presents certain ethical problems. For example, it would have been a misrepresentation not to include a minstrel show in our production because it was one of vaudeville's most popular components. But today, minstrelsy is rightly considered abhorrent; an insult to the African American community. And yet it represents a significant part of our cultural history. Minstrel shows were not only performed all over the United States but also as the first exported American entertainment, they toured the capitals of Europe to great acclaim. In minstrelsy it was common for white performers to put on blackface and enact the stereotypical behaviour of lazy black slaves. Black performers, in separate companies, also put on black make-up with white lips and performed the exaggerated stereotypes to enthusiastic houses worldwide.

This historical paradox provided us with a very specific challenge. We did not want to comment upon the material, or put a spin on it, or put quotation marks around the event. But we did want to light a fire under the enactment of the minstrel show with our own wakefulness and empathy. We encountered and channelled the issues by performing the stereotypes.

The most traumatic and emotional moments happened the first time the actors put on blackface make-up. This action was particularly macabre for the three African Americans in the cast. In front of long mirrors we watched each actor transform into a black-face/white-mouth arche-type. To apply the make-up, wear the costumes and enact the jokes, songs and dances, we faced and felt a piece of history. The audiences encountered a documentary embodi-ment, shapes of history filled with the reverberation of our actual engagement, sorrow and freedom. The result was powerful and reminded us in a living way of our own history. Through the embodiment of severe stereotypes, a small exorcism was performed.

⊂⊃

Another approach to stereotype requires a purer use of the body as a conduit to the past. Certain traditions around the world developed prescribed physical techniques to channel authentic experience through time. These formulas must be enacted without attempting to interpret them. The inter-action with these forms is purer than the distortion necessary with culturally abused stereotypes and the result is a feeling of rapture as emotions are channelled.

Lisa Wolford's remarkable book *Grotowski's Objective Drama Research*, about the work Polish director Jerzy Grotowski conducted at the University of California at Irvine, describes Grotowski's investigation of the American Shaker tradition. If the indigenous songs and dances of the Shakers are embodied properly, he proposed, the performers would channel authentic experience from the elusive tradition of the Shaker community. The relatively simple Shaker movements and tunes had to be performed without embellishment or interpretation, simply concentrating on the steps and melodies in order to allow the actor access to authentic Shaker experience.

The Japanese use the word *kata* to describe a prescribed set of movements that are repeatable. *Katas* can be found in acting, in cooking, in martial arts as well as in flower arrang-ing. The translation for the word *kata* in English is 'stamp', 'pattern' or 'mould'. In executing a *kata*, it is essential never to question its meaning but through the endless repetition the meaning starts to vibrate and acquire substance.

Americans are obsessed with freedom and often resent restrictions. I wonder if we have thought enough about the meaning of freedom? Do we mean the freedom to do or the freedom to be? Is it better to have the freedom to do anything we want any time we want, or to experience freedom as an internal liberty? Can you have both at the same time?

Perhaps we spend too much time concentrating on having the freedom to *do* what we want and proving that it is worthwhile. Perhaps we spend too much time avoiding *katas*, containers, clichés and stereotypes. If it is true that creativity occurs in the heat of spontaneous interaction with set forms, perhaps what is interesting is the quality of the heat you put under inherited containers, codes, and patterns of behaviour.

Many American actors are obsessed with the freedom to do whatever occurs to them in the moment. The notion of *kata* is abhorrent because, at first glance, it limits freedom. But everyone knows that in rehearsal you have to set *something*; you can either set *what* you are going to do or you can set *how* you will do it. To predetermine both *how* and *what* is tyranny and allows the actor no freedom. To fix neither makes it nearly impossible to intensify moments onstage through repetition. In other words, if you set too much, the results are lifeless. If you set too little, the results are unfocused.

So – if it is necessary to set something and also to leave something open, then the question arises, Do you set *what* is done or *how* it is done? Do you set the form or the content? Do you set the action or the emotion? Due to the pervasive American misunderstanding of the Stanislavsky system, rehearsals often become about eliciting strong emotions and then fixing those emotions. But human emotion is evanescent and ephemeral and setting the emotions cheapens the emotions. Therefore I believe that it is better to set the exterior (the form, the action) and allow the interior (the quality of being, the ever-altering emotional landscape) freedom to move and change in every repetition.

If you allow the emotions free rein to respond to the heat of the moment, then what you set is the form, the container, the *kata*. You work this way, not because you are ultimately most interested in form but, paradoxically, because you are most interested in the human experience. You move away from something in order to come closer to it. To allow for emotional freedom, you pay attention to form. If you embrace the notion of containers or *katas*, then your task is to set a fire, a human fire, inside these containers and start to burn.

⬭

Is it possible to meet one another fresh within the constraints of set form? Is it possible to burn through the inherited meanings of stereotype and unleash something fresh and share that with others?

A friend once described an incident in a crowded bus in San Francisco. She noticed two wildly disparate individuals pushed up close to each other on a narrow seat across from her: one a fragile elderly lady, and the second a flashy transvestite. Suddenly the bus lurched and the elderly lady's hair-net caught on to a ring on the transvestite's hand.

The moment the elderly lady's hair-net caught on to the transvestite's ring, the two were caught up in an exquisite mutual crisis. Forced by circumstances to deal with each other, the boundaries that normally defined and separated them dissolved instantly. Suddenly the potential for something new and fresh sprang into being. Perhaps one might express outrage, or possibly they would both burst out laughing. The boundaries evaporated and they found themselves without the cushion of definitions that had formerly sufficed to keep them separate.

When I heard this story, I jumped. It embodies an unmistakable lesson about what is possible between actors onstage and between actors and audience in a theatre.

The Japanese have a word to describe the quality of space and time between people: *ma'ai*. In the martial arts, the *ma'ai* is vital because of the danger of mortal attack. On the stage, the space between actors should also be continually endowed with quality, attention, potential and even danger. The *ma'ai* must be cultivated, respected and sharpened. The lines between actors on the stage should never go slack.

I spoke once with an actor who played Nick in *Who's Afraid of Virginia Woolf* with Glenda Jackson as Martha. He said that she never, ever, let the line between her and the other three actors go slack. The tendency with a lesser actor, playing a dissipated alcoholic character sliding into entropy, would be to loosen the tension and sink into the sofa. But with Jackson, the lines between her and the others had to be taut in every moment. Only when she left the stage did those lines loosen.

When approaching stereotype as an ally, you do not embrace a stereotype in order to hold it rigid; rather, you burn through it, undefining it and allowing human experience to perform its alchemy. You meet one another in an arena of potential transcendence of customary definitions. You awaken opposition and disagreement. If the character you are playing is dissipated and alcoholic you intensify the outward-directed energy. When you walk downstage you do not think about walking downstage; rather you think about not walking upstage. You wake up what is not. You mistrust assumed boundaries and definitions. You take care of the quality of space and time between youself and others. And you keep the channels open in order to embody the living history of inherited stereotypes.

⬭

Stereotypes are containers for memory, history and assumption. I once heard a theory about how culture infiltrates the human imagination. It starts with the notion that the average American's mental pictures of the French Revolution are the images from the musical *Les Miserables*, even for those who have never seen *Les Mis*. Culture is invasive and fluid. It moves through the air and saturates human experience.

To play Stanley Kowalski in *A Streetcar Named Desire*, do you pretend that Marlon Brando never played the character? What do you do with the stereotypes of the T-shirt and posturing? Do you avoid thinking about Brando or do you study his performance and use it? Do you try to arrive at a completely novel Kowalski? What do you do with the audience's memory?

When staging classics such as *Romeo and Juliet*, *Oedipus Rex* or *Singin' in the Rain*, how do you handle the public's shared memory? Can you include the baggage of a play's history in the *mise-en-scène*? What is our responsibility to the audience's own shared history of stereotype and cliché? What is supposed to happen on the receiving end?

It is very easy to make me cry. A boy running across a field towards his lost pet collie named Lassie can be a trigger mechanism for me. I'm like Pavlov's dog; I burst into tears. As an audience member, my big emotional triggers are loss and transformation.

It is actually not difficult to make everyone in any audience feel and think the same thing at the same time. It is not difficult to lock down meaning and manipulate response. What is trickier is to generate an event or a moment which will trigger many different possible meanings and associations. It takes craft to set up the circumstances that are simple and yet contain the ambiguities and the incongruity of human experience.

Should the whole audience feel and think the same thing at the same time or should each audience member feel and think something different at a different time? This is the fundamental issue that lies at the heart of the creative act: the artist's intentions vis-à-vis the audience.

Between the towns of Amherst and Northampton in western Massachusetts, two malls are situated right next to each other. Locally they are labelled the 'dead' mall and the 'live' mall. Both huge, one mall functions successfully, always full of activity and crowded stores, and the other, right next door, the dead one, is mostly empty and ghostlike, a visible failure. Both malls do have functioning multi-screen cineplexes, and film-goers are pretty much the only traffic the dead mall sees.

One summer afternoon during the summer that Stephen Spielberg released both *E.T.* and *Poltergeist*, I went to see *E.T.* at the dead mall. Because of the wild popularity of Spielberg's two films, it seemed that both malls, both cineplexes were showing either *E.T.* or *Poltergeist* in all their mini-theatres. As I watched the film I dutifully cried at the moments I was supposed to cry and walked out of the theatre at the end of the movie feeling small and insignificant and used. As I walked towards the parking lot, I could see thousands of other people exiting the theatres in both the dead mall and the live mall, all making a procession to their cars. The sun was setting, and as far as I could see there were cars full of Spielberg audiences making their way out towards the main highway. As I got into my car it was beginning to rain so I turned on the windshield wipers and headlights and saw thousands of other cars turning on their windshield wipers and headlights. Suddenly, watching this spectacle through the batting of the windshield wipers, I had the appalling sensation that each one of us, isolated in our separate cars and just having seen a Spielberg film, were feeling the same thing – not in a glorious communal sense that raises our hearts and spirits but rather, I felt, the film had made us smaller. We had been treated as mass consumers. We had been manipulated.

It is not difficult to trigger the same emotion in everyone. What is difficult is to trigger complex associations so that everyone has a different experience. Umberto Eco in his seminal book *The Open Text*, analyses the difference between closed and open text. In a closed text, there is one possible interpretation. In an open text, there can be many.

In the theatre we can choose to create moments in which everyone watching has a similar experience or moments which trigger different associations in everyone. Is our intention to impress the audience or to creatively empower them?

⊂⊃

Susan Sontag, in her essay 'Fascinating Fascism', explores the aesthetics of fascism through the life and work of Hitler's filmmaker Leni Riefenstahl. She proposes that fascist aesthetics flow from a preoccupation with situations of control, submissive behaviour, the manipulation of emotions and the repudiation of the intellect. Fascist art glorifies surrender and exalts mindlessness.

Several years ago I visited two places in Germany during the course of one week and experienced two completely different kinds of architecture. Both were built for masses of people but the intentions motivating the design were so different as to be revelatory when thinking about the audience's experience of an artist's work. One was the site of the Nuremberg rallies where Hitler held forth to the masses and the other was the vast complex in Munich that hosted the 1972 Winter Olympics.

In Nuremberg the architecture is huge and impressive and as I walked around the grounds I felt small and insignificant. The architecture was definitely preoccupied with control, submissive behaviour, manipulation of emotions and the repudiation of the intellect. The opposite experience awaited me in Munich at the Olympic Stadium. Despite the magnitude of the gigantic complex, everywhere I walked, I felt present and large. The architecture invited diverse responses and hypertextual wandering.

The Nazi Party's rally ground is a huge complex of assembly halls and stadiums on a site that conformed to what Hitler's architect Albert Speer called *Versammlungs-architektur* (assembly architecture). Related in function to Hitler's interest in mass psychology and how best to influence people en masse, Speer described the architecture as 'a means for stabilizing the mechanism of his domi-nation'. The architecture induced servitude by putting everyone in their place. The intention behind the design of this site was to make people feel small and for them to be impressed.

In Munich, by contrast, the grounds and buildings of the 1980 Winter Olympics, designed by the noted architect Frei Otto, is an open playful environment. One of his most beautiful achievements is the roof of the Olympic Stadium, astonishing in its grace and fluidity. Otto specializes in tensile architecture. Structures designed as tensile archi-tecture are created by tension, or pulling apart, in contrast to the more familiar, conventional architecture which is forged by compression. The buildings look like huge spidery tents. They are generous and asymmetrical and as you walk around them, the views constantly shift. The buildings and stadium lie gracefully over several hills and invite wandering and contemplation. Quite different from the fascist intention to control and subdue, these structures encourage people to move and think freely and creatively.

After the physical experience of these two contradictory expressions in architecture – one which unleashes the imagination and another which closes it down – I knew that I had to apply the lesson to my work as a director in the theatre. Do I want to create work in which everyone feels the same or everyone feels differently? Do I want the audience to feel small and manipulated or do I work towards something in which there is room for the audience to move around, imagine and make associations?

⬭

The paradox in an artist's relationship to an audience is that, in order to talk to many people, you must speak only to one, what Umberto Eco calls 'the model reader'. I learned about the model reader in the theatre after directing a play entitled *No Plays, No Poetry* . . . in 1988, based on the theoretical writings of Bertolt Brecht.

In New York City, around that time, a joke was circulating among the downtown theatre scene that downtown theatre people only made work for other downtown theatre people. In reaction to that bothersome notion, I always tried to throw as wide a net as I could in order to speak to the biggest, most diverse audience I could imagine. But with *No Plays, No Poetry* . . . I decided to go ahead and make a play for my friends. I wanted the play to serve as a love letter to the theatre community. At the end of the process, I always imagined an artist in the downtown theatre community as the receiver. I had no expectations of a wider public. Paradoxically, *No Plays, No Poetry* . . . became one of the most accessible works of theatre that I have ever directed. It spoke to many people because I chose one person to speak to. Since then, I have always pictured my model reader while preparing and rehearsing a play.

⬭

In the theatre we reach out and touch the past through literature, history and memory so that we might receive and relive significant and relevant human questions in the present and then pass them on to future generations. This is our function; this is our task. In light of that purpose, I want to think more positively about the usefulness of stereotypes and challenge my assumptions about originality. If we embrace rather than avoid stereotype, if we enter the container and push against its limits, we are testing our humanity and our wakefulness. The containers are powerful visual and audio stimuli for audiences and, if handled with great vigilance by the artist, can connect us with time.

embarrassment

SIX

● ● ● The leap, not the step, is what makes the experience possible.

(Heiner Müller)

Every creative act involves a leap into the void. The leap has to occur at the right moment and yet the time for the leap is never prescribed. In the midst of a leap, there are no guarantees. To leap can often cause acute embarrassment. Embarrassment is a partner in the creative act – a key collaborator. If your work does not sufficiently embarrass you, then very likely no one will be touched by it.

A friend of mine, an actor, harboured a life-long fantasy to be a rock star. Fuelled by his devotion to Sting, Mick Jagger and Peter Gabriel, he assembled a band, practised in a basement studio and finally got a booking in a club in the East Village in New York City. He invited me to the performance. The club was noisy, his band mediocre, and my friend's performance, unfortunately, was even worse.

Although he executed all the requisite rock star moves, the event had a remarkably false feel. He performed in front of three appropriately tough-looking back-up musicians and bombed.

At the end of the set, I turned to my companion, Annette Humpe, who actually *was* a rock star from Berlin, and asked her why the performance had been such a failure. She answered without hesitation: 'Er hat keine Scheu.' Roughly translated, 'Scheu' means shyness or embarrassment. 'He has no embarrassment.' I wanted to know more. 'He's an actor, not a singer,' she explained. 'He is performing a singer, but he's not really singing.'

In order to identify the characteristics of an authentic singer, Annette Humpe suggested that we stay on in the club to hear the next band. The following group featured a woman who simply stood in front of her band and sang. At first she seemed awkward and unsophisticated but very soon it became apparent that she was, in fact, a real singer. The act of singing, the intensity of the sound emanating from her body increased her vulnerability. Her own self-awareness disconcerted her and she appeared slightly embarrassed.

If one is not 'touched' by the brashness of what is expressed *through* you, then, as Gertrude Stein remarked about Oakland, California, 'there is no there there.' Perhaps Judy Garland raised her arms into what became the iconic Garland shape from her sense of embarrassment and self-awareness. From that moment onward, singers and drag queens imitated the exact movement of her arms in heedless adoration. But most of these performers also manage to avoid her original embarrassment. It is true that there are a few great drag queens who have appropriated Judy Garland's shapes and managed to transcend the inherited stereotypes. A great 'repeater' uses the original pattern, not to imitate mindlessly, but rather to open new frontiers.

In the case of a mediocre performer who executes mindless imitation, the discomfiture of the original creative moment is missing. In search of authenticity, one cannot expect to find security and safety inside inherited forms, plays, songs or movements. What's necessary is to rekindle the fire inside of repetition and be prepared for a personal exposure to its effects. Be prepared to be embarrassed.

⊂⊃

● ● ● Acting is half shame, half glory. Shame at exhibiting yourself, glory when you can forget yourself.

(John Gielgud)

Usually we think of embarrassment as self-consciousness, shame or awkwardness. But the etymology of the word suggests other useful possibilities. It first appeared in 1672 and derives from the French *embarrasser*, which means to entangle, obstruct or trouble; to encumber; impede, to make difficult or intricate; to complicate. In Portuguese, *barras* is a bar or an obstruction. An *embarrass* is an obstruction to navigation in a stream, caused by the lodging of driftwood or trunks of trees. Embarrassment, in this sense, means to hinder, complicate and impede.

I like to think of embarrassment as an obstruction we encounter that helps us clarify our mission. Can we welcome the entanglement of engagement? Can we allow our sense of authority to be challenged in the encounter? When you grapple with something that is just out of your reach, you find yourself entangled in something that you haven't yet mastered.

Embarrassment is a teacher. A good actor risks embarrassment in every moment. There is nothing more thrilling than to be in rehearsal with an actor who is willing to set foot into embarrassing territory. The uneasiness keeps the lines tight. If you try to avoid being embarrassed by what you do, nothing will happen because the territory remains safe and unexposed. Embarrassment engenders a glow and a presence and a dissolving of habit.

To avoid embarrassment is a natural human tendency. Feeling truly exposed to others is rarely a comforting sensation. But if what you do or make does not embarrass you sufficiently, then it is probably not personal or intimate enough. Revelation is necessary to warrant attention. The feeling of embarrassment is a good omen because it signifies that you are meeting the moment fully, with an openness to the new feelings it will engender.

The best way to avoid embarrassment is to treat the material at hand as a known entity rather than an unknown one. As a director I can choose to approach a play either with the attitude that it is a small controllable canvas or a huge canvas, brimming with untapped potential. If I choose to possess a superior attitude to the material, it will conform, remain safe and unthreatening. It will stay smaller than me. If I adopt the attitude that the project is an adventure larger than anything I might imagine, an entity that will challenge me to find an instinctual path through it, the project will be allowed its proper magnitude.

When cast in a particular role, an actor also faces a choice of attitude. If she or he chooses to consider the character as someone whose vistas are beyond their own limited experience, the results will be remarkably different from those of someone who decides to see their character as smaller than themselves. The first will undergo a greater, more personal adventure and, consequently, more necessary embarrassment. The actor who decides to consider the character smaller than him- or herself will rarely attempt anything not already familiar. In rehearsal she or he will inevitably utter the dreaded words: 'My character would never do that.' This small-minded attitude leads to a tight, controlled, and ultimately uninteresting performance. The attitude which allows for the character to be larger than one's own experience results in an adventure of unlimited possibility.

After acting in a play for an entire year, Vanessa Redgrave realized that there were parts of the production she just did not know how to do, so she decided to let her not-knowing show while she worked it out. She hoped that audiences would either look the other way so that she could figure it out, or, if they wanted to look, that would be OK too. As it turned out, these moments were absolutely riveting. I imagine that the force of her not-knowing cut through the evening. I imagine that she felt more exposed, more vulnerable and, probably, more present and awake.

The enemy of art is *assumption*: the assumption that you know what you are doing, the assumption that you know how to walk and how to talk, the assumption that what you 'mean' will mean the same thing to those who receive it. The instant you make an assumption about who the audience is or what the moment is, that moment will be asleep. Assumptions can prevent you from entering new and embarrassing territory.

If you manage to question your assumptions, you will find yourself instantly, childlike, face to face with new sensations. Even the people around you, untamed by your assumptions, will suddenly seem fresh and full of potential. In the midst of this new territory you get inspired, you get defeated, you feel embarrassment.

In the process of studying the necessary distress of embarrassment, I found ten helpful notions to get through the tough moments.

1 You cannot hide; your growth as an artist is not separate from your growth as a human being: it is all visible

●●● The only possible spiritual development (for an artist) is in the sense of depth. The artistic tendency is not expansive, but a contraction. And art is the apotheosis of solitude.

(Samuel Beckett)

As a young director, I was so thrilled when Meredith Monk, whom I admired tremendously, came to see a production I had directed. Anxious afterwards to know what she thought, I pursued her for a critique. She said that the play needed more interval, more space, more silence.

I jumped at this. Her criticism made sense and I wanted to do something about it. How can I get more interval in my work, I wondered? Finally, after much consideration, I realized that I couldn't just impose more interval into my work; I had to *have* more interval, more space, more silence in me.

A director cannot hide from an audience because intentions are always visible, palpable. An audience senses your attitude towards them. They smell your fright or condescension. They know instinctively that you want only to impress or conquer. They sense your engagement or lack of it. These qualities live in your body and are visible in your work. You must have a reason to do what it is you do because these reasons are felt by anyone who comes in contact with your work. It matters how you treat people, how you take responsibility in a crisis, what values you develop, your politics, what you read, how you speak and even which words you choose. You cannot hide.

Neither can an actor hide from an audience. Japanese director Tadashi Suzuki once remarked: 'There is no such thing as good or bad acting, only degrees of profundity of the actor's reason for being on stage.' This reason is manifest in your body and in your energy. First you have to have a reason to act and then, in order to articulate clearly, you must be courageous in that act. The quality of any moment on the stage is determined by the vulnerability and modesty one feels in relation to that courageous, articulate, necessary act.

What you do in rehearsal is visible in the product. The quality of the time spent together is visible. The chief ingredient in rehearsal is real, personal interest. And interest is one of the few components in theatre that has absolutely nothing to do with artifice. You cannot fake interest. It must be genuine. Interest is your engine and it determines the lengths to which you will travel in the heat of engagement. It is also an ingredient that vacillates and changes in time. You have to be sensitive to its vicissitudes.

In rehearsal, a director cannot hide from an actor. Again, intentions are visible and palpable. An actor can sense the quality of interest and attentiveness the director brings into the room. It is real and it is tangible. If intentions are cheap, the actor knows this. The line between the director and the actor is undeniable and it can be either tense or slack. A director should attend to that line with interest and listening.

In art, the truth is always manifest in the experience of it. The audience will finally have the most direct experience of the breadth or lack of your interest. They will feel the truth about your intentions and about who you are, who you have become. They will instinctively know what you are up to. It is all visible.

2 Every creative act includes a leap

●●● Art serves us best precisely at that point where it can shift our sense of what is possible, when we know more than we knew before, when we feel we have – by some manner of a leap – encountered the truth. That, by the logic of art, is always worth the pain.

(T.S. Eliot)

In rehearsal and in performance, a leap is required at every juncture. Every time an actor walks on to the stage, she or he must be prepared to leap unexpectedly. Without that willingness, the stage will remain a tame and conventional place. Be prepared to leap at the appropriate moment and you will never know when the moment will be appropriate. The door opens and you must go through it with no consideration for the consequences. You leap. But you must also accept that the leap itself does not guarantee anything. And it does not mitigate the embarrassment; rather, it heightens it.

According to Rollo May in his book *The Courage to Create*, artists and scientists throughout history agree that, at their best, they feel as though they are being spoken *through*. They have somehow managed to get out of their own way. Some say that God speaks through them. Others maintain, in a more pedestrian fashion, that in order to get out of their own way and bypass the frontal lobe of the brain, they go for a walk in the forest or take a nap. They have to get their mind *off* what they are trying to do in order to make the most inspired connections. The mind is always out to ambush the process. The discoveries and break-throughs happen when you successfully manage to get out of your own way.

I spend many hours in libraries and with research materials for every play I direct. At one time I thought that the aimless meandering around the libraries and the little naps that I took while doing research were pure laziness. I wandered and slept. I assumed guiltily that I was avoiding the necessary rigour of study. But, it turns out that this wandering served to get me out of my own way and make space for necessary fuzzy logic conceptual leaps.

In preparation for a production of Georg Büchner's *Danton's Death*, I studied the French Revolution to get a sense of the energy behind the play's genesis. I was also looking for an arena it might inhabit and a way to channel that fierce energy. In the library I sporadically meandered away from the books on the French Revolution, took naps, wandered through the stacks and flipped through magazines. One afternoon, in a kind of a daze, I found my-self leafing through a new book on clubs in downtown New York City by Michael Musto, a writer for the *Village Voice*. At that time, in the mid-1980s, a big, vibrant club movement swept the downtown scene. These clubs sometimes set up special environments on a particular theme. An array of young people who called themselves 'celebutants' dressed wildly, danced, partied and took drugs in these themed clubs. One club, Area, spent an entire month on a French Revolution theme. The celebutants dressed and behaved accordingly.

Suddenly, the arena for *Danton's Death* jumped out of the pages of Michael Musto's book. I made a big conceptual leap. During the bloodiest part of the French Revolution, around 1795, the mad energy of violence and change engendered a movement of vigilantes called 'the Gilded Youth'. Some were released prisoners, some were draft-dodgers, many were clerks and petty bureaucrats, and all were looking for trouble. Affecting extravagant clothes and hairstyles, they danced and partied, making it their business to harass, disrupt and break up public occasions.

I took a conceptual leap. What would happen, I wondered, if we staged the entire play in the context of a club. The parallel of the celebutants and the 'Gilded Youth' might channel the necessary energy needed to give the play resonance. What would happen if the actors played modern-day celebutants who became 'Gilded Youth' to spin out the wild rollercoaster ride of the play with all its big political speeches, scheming and bloodshed?

This leap provided and 'in' for me and for the actors and designers. It gave us a place to start. This leap became the trampoline upon which we could enter the play and a context in which the actors could meet one another through the fiction of the characters and situations. I think the audience enjoyed the ride.

3 You cannot create results; you can only create the conditions in which something might happen

It is not the director's responsibility to produce results but, rather, to create the circumstances in which something might happen. The results come about by themselves. With one hand firmly on the specifics and one hand reaching to the unknown, you start to work.

I know that at certain key moments I have to keep out of the actors' way. Not infrequently when an actor is working on the most difficult moments in a play, I know that I should concentrate on other things. I should give space so that they might to do their own work.

I directed Elmer Rice's big expressionist play *The Adding Machine* at Actors Theater of Louisville. The character Zero, played by Bill McNulty, has a huge monologue in a courtroom where he ensnares himself in front of a jury. His five-page monologue constitutes the entire scene and it is very tricky to navigate. I knew that Bill needed room to roam, to explore, to find the necessary channels of self-revelation that the play asked for. He needed room to follow a scent. And he didn't need me to add to the pressure that already existed for him in the scene. And so, in rehearsal, I concentrated on everything on the stage except him. I kept the scene moving but used the time to refine the positioning of the jury and take care of spacing issues. I let him do his work. If I had put all my concentration directly on him at that time in rehearsal, I know that he would probably have got shut down by my desire for him to find his way in the scene. My intention was for Bill to find his way, but I got at that intention by concentrating on other things. For someone watching the rehearsal it probably would have looked like I had no interest in the character Zero. But in fact the opposite was true. Sometimes, you have to go through the back door to get to the front.

Rehearsal is not about forcing things to happen; rather, rehearsal is about listening. The director listens to the actors. The actors listen to one another. You listen collectively to the text. You listen for clues. You keep things moving. You probe. You do not gloss over moments as if they were understood. Nothing is understood. You bring your attention to the situation as it evolves. I think of rehearsal like playing the Ouija board, where you collectively put your hands on a question and then follow the movement as it starts to unfold. You follow it until the scene reveals its secret.

By taking care of the circumstances in which you are working, things start, inevitably, to happen. Quantum physics suggests that nothing is at rest. Nothing stops. Ever. There is always movement. Ours is an observer-created reality. The act of observing something changes it. The Taoists advise: 'To do the not to do.' The active not doing. Be awake and ride the events as they occur. The effort to force something to happen makes listening impossible.

To arrive at a place where something sufficiently embarrassing can happen, I place my attention on the circumstances of the rehearsal. I attend to the quality of the room, including punctuality, lack of clutter and cleanliness. As we start to rehearse, I concentrate on details. Often it doesn't matter which details, but my act of concentration helps to concentrate everything and everybody else. I try to be present as fully as possible, listen with my whole body and then respond instinctively to what happens. The creative process happens by itself.

4 To enter paradise you usually have to go through the back door

One of the greatest essays about the theatre, entitled 'About a Marionette Theater', written by Heinrich von Kleist in 1812, addresses the issues of affectation, self-consciousness and embarrassment in the theatre. Kleist meets his friend, a ballet master, who takes him through a process of thinking about how the affected behaviour we encounter on the stage emerges from the actor's hyper-awareness of him- or herself in action. The lack of naturalness arises out of self-consciousness. Since the fall of Adam and Eve, concludes the essay, since the origin of self-consciousness, we cannot enter paradise through the front gate. We have to go around to the back of the world.

What does Kleist mean? Is he referring to the self-consciousness of embarrassment? Does he mean that we cannot be natural on stage just by trying to be natural on stage? I reread this essay regularly because of its common sense and insight into one of the major problems we face every time we try to do something on the stage.

Haven't we all experienced genuine moments of inspiration where natural genius seems to flow naturally through us? But then, how quickly does that state of grace pass! How do we repeat the discoveries without affectation? How do we create the conditions for God to speak through us on a regular basis? Most of the time self-consciousness gets in our way. As soon as you start to stretch the boundaries of habit or work on the outer edges of your capabilities, an acute self-consciousness immediately sets in which can feel completely disconcerting and unproductive. This obstacle, this self-consciousness lives with us in almost everything that we do.

Julian Jaynes in his book *The Origin of Consciousness in the Breakdown of the Bicameral Man*, places the beginning of self-consciousness in Western civilization at around 1400 BC, during the Minoan period in Greece. He maintains that the human brain split into a right and left hemisphere as part of the biological necessity to maintain hegemony in a world growing more and more complex. This notion of the left and right hemispheres of the brain can be equated with the Fall of Adam and Eve and the birth of the obstacle self-consciousness. After eating from the tree of knowledge, Adam and Eve, suddenly conscious of their nakedness, felt modest and covered themselves. Suddenly they were embarrassed.

The part of the brain that can easily divert you from your path is commonly known as the frontal lobe. It generates the constant buzzing in your head that wants to censure you and is out to ambush your every move. In order to find a creative flow you have to give the frontal lobe something else to do so that it will stay out of your way. You have to engage that part of the brain with busywork so that it will be otherwise engaged. Only then, once you have found your way around the obstacle of the pervasive buzzing, can you start to follow an aesthetic scent or a creative whim. Only then can you begin to trust in your instincts. Then, once you are free to be spontaneous, intuition can be your guide.

During his life, Stanislavsky found systems to engage the frontal lobe of the actor's brain. He too must have understood that in order to enter paradise you have to go through the back door. He invented useful mechanisms of distraction (the back door) to get yourself out of your own way in order to attain spontaneity and naturalness (paradise) on the stage. He gave these useful diversions names like 'given circumstances', 'motivation', 'justification', 'the Magic If', 'objectives and super-objectives', etc.

How do you get out of your own way? First, accept the paradox that theatre is artifice yet our search is for authenticity – art, as Picasso said, is the lie that tells the truth. Despite the artifice we search for spontaneity and freedom. But to enter that paradise, you cannot enter through the front gates; you must go around to the back door.

An actor knows that in order to muster a genuinely unaffected moment on the stage, she or he cannot simply try to be genuine. It's never as simple as that. No more than we could, say, play the violin genuinely without struggling with craft. The actor grapples with this issue on a daily basis by learning to handle the artifice through training and practice. Good actors know intuitively that they are half marionette and the rest is real inspiration, intuitive intelligence and listening. They concentrate on negotiating the artifice – the size of the stage, the blocking, the text, the costumes, the lights – to the point where the conscious mind – that is out to ambush us and make us small – is occupied with something else so that the spontaneity and naturalness can arrive unimpeded.

To find a way to approach *Danton's Death*, I had to find the back door – the celebutants in a club – to find a conduit to the authentic original energy of the play. You cannot look directly at the sun because it will injure your eyes, so you look to the side with the intention of experiencing the sun. Something unaffected might happen when we concentrate not on the thing itself, but on a thing to the side.

A working artist is in a constant struggle with the brain's attempts to ambush their work through diversion. Do not be seduced by the buzz. In all the work with artifice, while going through the back door, keep your inner eye secretly on paradise. Stay true to a deeper pursuit.

5 Allow yourself to go off balance

Most people become highly creative in the midst of an emergency. In the instant of imbalance and pressure, quick and decent solutions to big immediate problems must be found. It is in these moments of crisis that native intelligence and intuitive imagination kicks in: the woman who lifts a car because her child is trapped beneath, an inspired strategic choice in the crisis of battle, the quick decisions in the heat of a final rehearsal before a first night audience. I have found that, creatively, imbalance is more fruitful than stability.

Art begins in the struggle for equilibrium. One cannot create from a balanced state. Being off balance produces a predicament that is always interesting on stage. In the moment of imbalance, our animal instincts prompt us to struggle towards equilibrium and this struggle is endlessly engaging and fruitful. When you welcome imbalance into your work, you will find yourself instantly face to face with your own inclination towards habit. Habit is an artist's opponent. In art, the unconscious repetition of familiar territory is never vital or exciting. We must try to remain awake and alive in the face of our inclinations towards habit. Finding yourself off balance provides you with an invitation to disorientation and difficulty. It is not a comfortable prospect. You are suddenly out of your element and out of control. And it is here the adventure begins. When you welcome imbalance, you will instantly enter new and uncharted territory in which you feel small and inadequate in relation to the task at hand. But the fruits of this engagement abound.

6 Insecurity is OK

●●● I am mortified to be on the stage, but then again, it's the only place where I'm happy.

(Bob Dylan)

A director's job is not to supply answers but rather to provide interest. You need to find the right questions and discern when and how to ask them. If you already have the answers, then what is the point of being in rehearsal? But you certainly need to know what you are looking for.

Interest is the artist's primary tool and it occupies the territory of personal insecurity – you do not have the answers and you are provoked by the questions. You will occasionally be embarrassed by the search in the dark because of what you bump into. The engine for interest is curiosity. A director asks simple and meaningful questions propelled by curiosity. Curiosity cannot be faked. In the exquisite moments of curiosity and interest, we live in-between, we travel outward with inquiry. Interest is a feeling directed outward to an object or a person or a subject, a theme, or a play. In travelling outward, in pursuing an interest, we experience insecurity. Insecurity is not only OK, it is a necessary ingredient.

7 Use accidents

Things always go 'wrong'. Things happen that you haven't planned for. Sigmund Freud suggested that there is no such thing as an accident. Might an accident be a sign? Might it be asking for attention? An accident contains energy – the energy of uncontrolled shapes.

Normally when things start to fall apart we pull back. We want to reassess. Can this impulse be reversed? Can we welcome the energy of an accidental occurrence? In the moment that things start to fall apart can we enter into the event rather than shy away from it?

In rehearsal for a production of *Moby Dick*, the extra-ordinary actor George Kahn got so frustrated that he literally ran up a wall. The director Ric Zank instructed Kahn to 'keep it'. Many directors would have taken the frustration and the running up the wall as a cue to sit down and discuss the incident and the problem. Instead, Zank incorporated into the production what many would have considered inappropriate. And it worked for the play. It was such a difficult physical act that every time Kahn had to run up the wall in that particular moment in performance, he was forced to summon all of his strength and capability to accomplish it. If there is no such thing as an accident and everything is fodder and happens for a reason, then accidents can be channelled into the shape of a production. And these shapes contain energy, memory and necessary ambiguity.

I know a designer who loves it when someone bumps accidentally into the model for his scenic design because it always allows him to look at the elements he has been working with in an entirely new way.

8 Walk the tightrope between control and chaos

If your work is too controlled, it has no life. If it is too chaotic, no one can see or hear it.

In rehearsal, you have to set something, agree upon something. If you predetermine everything, if too much is agreed upon, there will be nothing left to the inspiration of the moment in performance. Some aspects of the process need to be left entirely alone. Controlling too much usually means that there is not enough trust of the actor's spontaneity and the audience's ability to contribute to the event.

W. C. Fields said 'never work with children or animals'. What he meant is that both children and animals are entirely uncontrollable entities and thus are almost always more interesting to watch than whatever planned moments are happening in conjunction with them. But the most exciting work has both: the carefully set moments and then something else that is entirely uncontrollable and full of potential.

9 Do your homework and know when to stop doing your homework

In every creative process there comes the moment where you have to stop worrying about whether or not you know enough about the subject you've been studying. A rehearsal is not about proving that what you have worked out before is the right solution for the play. The research eventually gets in your way. If you don't get beyond the homework, the outcome will become academic. Academic art simply validates the research. It does not challenge it.

In rehearsal you must be vigilant. You must listen with your whole being. In these heated moments, you cannot afford to think things through. You must be available and attentive to the doors that open unexpectedly. You must leap at the appropriate moment. You cannot wait. The doors close fast.

Study, analyse, free associate, conceptualize, prepare 150 ideas for every scene, write everything down and then be ready to throw it all away. It is important to prepare and it is important to know when to stop preparing. You will never be ready and you must always be ready for this step. Your preparation gets you to the first step. And then something else takes over.

A Russian director once said to me, 'The most difficult part of the rehearsal process is the moment the actors must get up from the table where all the enchanting research and discussions have taken place, and begin to implement it on the stage. No one wants to move away from the comfort of the table, but,' he said, 'I will show you a trick, a director's trick that will ensure that the actors will want to act.' He then demonstrated the trick. We were, at that moment, sitting together at a table. 'Imagine that we are at a table with a group of actors, studying a play,' he said and then picked up his chair where he and I had been seated together and moved it away from me to a certain distance. Then he placed the chair down and started to look at me intently. I felt exposed. 'No actors actually want to perform their scene sitting around a table.' By moving away he created a stage and with his gaze he suggested the exquisite pressure of an audience's attention. Suddenly the comfort of gathering around discussing ideas was replaced with the rapt attention of a man who looks at you and says 'show me'.

10 Concentrate on detail

When in doubt, when you are lost, don't stop. Instead, concentrate on detail. Look around, find a detail to concentrate on and do that. Forget the big picture for a while. Just put your energy into the details of what is already there. The big picture will eventually open up and reveal itself if you can stay out of the way for a while. It won't open up if you stop. You have to stay involved but you don't always have to stay involved with the big picture.

While paying attention to the details and welcoming insecurity, while walking the tightrope between control and chaos and using accidents, while allowing yourself to go off balance and going through the back door, while creating the circumstances in which something might happen and being ready for the leap, while not hiding and being ready to stop doing homework, something is bound to happen. And it will probably be appropriately embarrassing.

resistance

>
> Since the artist cares in a particular way for the phase of experience in which union is achieved, he does not shun moments of resistance and tension. He rather cultivates them, not for their own sake but because of their potentialities, bringing to living consciousness an experience that is unified and total.
>
> (John Dewey)

Every act generates resistance to that act. To sit down to write almost always requires a personal struggle against the resistance to write. Entropy and inertia are the norm. To meet and overcome resistance is a heroic act that requires courage and a connection to a reason for the action.

Invited to deliver six lectures as part of Harvard's Norton Lecture Series, writer Italo Calvino decided to meditate on qualities he valued in art. Unfortunately Calvino died before completing the final lecture but they were published as a beautiful little book entitled *Six Memos for the Next*

Millennium. Each lecture constitutes a chapter on each of the six qualities he loved in art: lightness, quickness, exactitude, visibility, multiplicity and continuity.

Life, Calvino proposes, naturally pulls us down towards decay and finally, death. Our struggle to create is a fight against the weight and slowness of our own decay. To him, the distinction and force of art is in its intrinsic lightness and visibility, its quickness, multiplicity and exactitude. It rises above the resistance against it.

The action of pushing against resistance is a daily act and can also be considered a necessary ingredient in the creative process – an ally. How we measure ourselves against the natural resistances we encounter every day determines the quality of what we accomplish.

I arrived in New York City after finishing undergraduate school with a commitment to direct plays. But no theatre in town was willing to take a risk on a young untested woman director. Faced with this immediate resistance, the task was obvious. I had to create the circumstances for myself in which I might direct. I had to produce as well as direct. This was a terrifying obstacle and it called upon all my strength and imagination. Faced with this explicit resistance and armed with determination, I scoped out the territory. I asked a friend how one would find actors to work with. He suggested I put an ad in the weekly newspaper *Backstage*. I did. It read, 'Actors interested in an investigation of assassination and murder using Shakespeare's *Macbeth*, please call . . .' In the ad I neglected to mention that I had no money to pay and no organization to produce. But the phone started ringing and then it didn't stop. It felt like opening Pandora's Box and looking into the indisputable daily plight of the New York City actor. Due to the volume of calls, to this day I am shy of the telephone. It was overwhelming. When I nervously mentioned the lack of money on the phone, many hung up. But about 200 actors wanted to audition anyway. Because I was too frightened to conduct conventional auditions, I invited each actor to come for an interview and then to read aloud from a Sylvia Plath poem. I sat behind a makeshift table in my home, holding tightly onto it so that no one would notice that I was shaking with fear and anxiety. I vividly remember one actor, twice my age, handing me a resumé which listed his extensive experience on Broadway, off Broadway, film, television and commercials. His breath smelled faintly of alcohol and he started to weep as he implored me to engage him: 'I just want to do something meaningful,' he said.

In those early years in New York I did create dozens of shows with actors who were willing to work for the love of it. I learned how to make theatre happen under difficult circumstances. We staged plays on rooftops, in store-front windows, in basements, in clubs, wherever we could find a place to perform. I learned how to use architecture as the set design and how to work with many different kinds of actors, each with a distinct need. I met people who were as determined as I to make theatre happen and who took on huge responsibilities to help to accomplish my projects. I believe that if I have a career in the theatre today it is because I managed to use the obstacles and resistances that life offered in those early years. I learned to use the given circumstances, whatever they might be.

These experiences taught me to appreciate the resistances that life offers and to recognize them as an ally. There will always be resistances and obstacles no matter what the situation. Whether at a huge subsidized theatre or a tiny community theatre, in a city or in the countryside, something or someone will always present resistance. The question becomes: how can you use the difficulties and obstacles to help rather than discourage expression?

$$\bigcirc$$

●●● To write a work of genius is almost always a feat of prodigious difficulty. Everything is against the likelihood that it will come from the writer's mind whole and entire. Generally material circumstances are against it. Dogs will bark; people will interrupt; money must be made; health will break down. Further, accentuating all these difficulties and making them harder to bear is the world's notorious indifference. It does not ask people to write poems and novels and histories; it does not need them.

(Virginia Woolf)

If resistances are a daily given and a necessary ingredient to the flow of creativity and life, what is the best way to work with them? Here are a few ideas: first, recognize that the resistances that present themselves will immediately intensify your commitment and generate energy in the endeavour. Resistance demands thought, provokes curiosity and mindful alertness, and, when overcome and utilized, eventuates in elation. Ultimately the quality of any work is reflected in the size of obstacles encountered. If one's attitude is right, joy, vigour and break-throughs will be the results of resistance met rather than avoided.

Michelangelo chose one of the greatest possible creative obstacles when he pointed to the ceiling in the Sistine Chapel and resolved to paint there. The resistance was tremendous and the results, which we can experience today, are an example of heightened articulation in the face of colossal difficulty. Beethoven was almost completely deaf when he wrote his most complex quartets. The literal physical obstacles, when met with the right kind of spirit, can produce astonishing results. The calibre of the obstacle determines the quality of the expression.

As a young director, I began every new project by inviting the actors and everyone involved with a project to brain-storm ideas together. Inspired by Edward DeBono's writing on the subject, we called these sessions 'lateral thinking'. Freely associating off one another's ideas, we engendered a collective image of the world of the play and imagined together what could happen in that arena. We always dreamed up elaborate plans and wonderful imagery that, in fact, we had no way of paying for. The constraints of a non-existent budget and severely condensed rehearsal times never allowed for the sixteen motorcycles we envisioned crossing the stage at a particular moment in the production. Instead, we would end up with one bicycle because that is what we could find for free. Because we usually did not even have a real theatre at our disposal we would perform on a deserted construction site or a community centre. Because we all had to work day jobs, we were forced by circumstances to compress our rehearsals into late-night hours in loaned rooms. Despite these restrictions, we did achieve theatre with presence and energy so, after a while, I was invited to direct in real theatres with real budgets.

When I did start getting real budgets and when the opportunities for design elements and technical support became available to me, I found that I had to be very careful because, if things came too easily, the results were not always best for the play. If there are not enough obstacles in a given process, the result can lack rigour and depth.

Resistance heightens and magnifies the effort. Meeting a resistance, confronting an obstacle, or overcoming a difficulty always demands creativity and intuition. In the heat of the conflict, you have to call on new reserves of energy and imagination. You develop your muscles in the act of overcoming resistance – your artist muscles. Like a dancer, you have to practise regularly to keep up muscularity. The magnitude of the resistances you choose to engage determines the progression and depth of your work. The larger the obstacles, the more you will transform in the effort.

⬭

●●● There is no expression without excitement, without turmoil. Yet an inner agitation that is discharged at once in a laugh or cry, passes away with its utterance. To discharge is to get rid of, to dismiss; to express is to stay by, to carry forward in development, to work out to completion. A gush of tears may bring relief, a spasm of destruction may give outlet to inward rage. But where there is no administration of objective conditions, no shaping of materials in the interest of embodying the excitement, there is no expression. What is sometimes called an act of self-expression might better be termed one of self-exposure; it discloses character – or lack of character – to others. In itself, it is only a spewing forth.

(John Dewey)

Art is expression. It requires creativity, imagination, intuition, energy and thought to take the random feelings of uneasiness and dissatisfaction and compress them into useful expression. An artist learns to concentrate rather than get rid of the daily discord and restlessness. It is possible to turn the irritating mass of daily frustrations into fuel for beautiful expression.

But in the moments of discord and discomfort, in the instant that we feel challenged by the circumstances, our natural inclination is to stop. Don't stop. Try to allow for the necessary discomfort generated by the struggle with the present circumstances. Use this discomfort as a stimulus for expression by concentrating it.

There is no expression without excitement, without turmoil. In the rapture of an emotion or in the discomfort of irritation, I am confronted with a choice: I can either immediately discharge the feelings or I can concentrate them, cook them and, in the appropriate moment, use them to express something.

Discharge is uncompressed. It erupts from the body without any filtering. It is not artful. It is random complaint. An inner agitation that is immediately discharged without compression, like a laugh or cry or random violence, disappears as it is invoked. The discharge may bring relief and self-exposure, but it is only a spewing forth. Nothing will have been wrought.

Compression makes expression possible. Without compression there is no ex-pression. Expression happens only after compression. Expression is the result of containing, shaping and embodying the excitement that boils up inside of you. The Japanese word *tameru* in Noh drama defines the action of holding back, of retaining.

●●● When you feel ten in your heart, express seven.

(Zeami)

A rehearsal is always about relationships, about being in the room together with other people, working towards something. The circumstances of a rehearsal inevitably conjures up difficult and contrary emotions in me. So, naturally, my emotions can become interpersonal, and interpersonal means personal. If I allow myself impulsively or randomly to discharge these emotions as they occur, the discharge can ruin the quality of the relationships and can interrupt the necessary channelling of a play. In every moment in rehearsal I am confronted with a choice: I can splatter my feelings around the room, or I can concentrate them and let them cook until the appropriate moment in which I might express an opinion or sentiment that is backed by this concentration of thought and feeling. This concentration and then the resulting expression is creative and supports the actors' efforts.

An actor is faced with a similar dilemma – the choice to discharge or concentrate experience. It is easy to discharge. You just let it go, spill it, whenever you feel overcome. But I believe that a good actor understands the necessity to concentrate the irritations, the random feelings, the difficulties, the infatuations, everything that occurs from moment to moment, and compress them, let them cook and find the appropriate moments for clear and articulate expression.

How does this work practically? First, as previously stated, start by welcoming the resistance and obstacles as a creative ally. The ensuing encounter with these invited obstacles inevitably causes personal discord and disharmony. The problem is a creative one to solve and leads to expression and articulation. For example, if an actor attempts to make a difficult task appear easy to an audience, the difficulty instantly creates resistances and conflict inside the actor's body. The problem demands compression of discord and then articulation of ease.

It is actually more challenging to find the necessary resistance for an 'easy' task than a difficult task. But it is just as necessary. Sitting in a chair, for example, might be considered easy. How do you create resistance, or something physical, unbeknownst to the audience, to push against while sitting in a chair? Actors know that pushing against a wall sometimes can help make speaking a text clearer, more urgent. Can you figure out how to create the same obstacle or resistance and urgency while simply standing onstage or sitting in a chair while speaking the text? The actor has to build a sense of conflict or resistance in the body.

Actors can also use one another to generate necessary creative resistance. Just the force of another person's presence offers something to push against. And the outward-directed energy between performers engenders good resilient tautness.

Canadian singer k. d. lang learned a life-altering lesson from Roy Orbison. As they worked together on a version of his song 'Cryin'', she recognized his artistic secret and tried it out herself. The result was a transformation of the gawky hyperactive younger k. d. into the mature, condensed performer she became after her collaboration with Orbison. From him she learned the potent combination of physical containment and emotional expansion.

The compression into restricted space and the patience demanded for this containment actually intensifies the life which is revealed in a minimum of activity. Try to develop an ability to keep energy in, to concentrate an action into limited space.

⬯

Laziness, impatience and distraction are three constant resistances that we face in almost every moment of our waking life. How we handle these three real enemies determines the clarity and force of our achievements.

Distraction is an *external* enemy. The temptation to be diverted by outside stimulus is an obstacle to be found everywhere. We live in a culture that surrounds us with invitations to distraction and a lot of people get rich from our desire for diversion. We are encouraged to switch channels, shop, cruise by, surf, call someone up or take a break.

In a speech at George Washington University in 1993, Vaclav Havel, the President of the Czech Republic, described his life as an imprisoned dissident in communist-run Czechoslovakia. He looks back at those years of the communist regime as a challenge, 'a challenge to think and to act'. While not wishing for communism's return, Havel salvaged something it taught him in his resistance to it. Today we live within another kind of totalitarianism. Each of us is a target of the attack machinery of consumerism. A media-drenched culture aims aggressively at our psyches with a constancy that breaks and numbs the spirit. This dangerous environment offers us an opportunity: the challenge to think and to act.

Laziness and impatience are constant *internal* resistances and they are very personal. We are all lazy. We are all impatient. Neither are evil qualities; rather, they are issues that we learn to handle properly and act on at the right moments. We navigate them in our aim towards expression.

●●● There are no such things as problems, only situations.

(Christo)

Attitude is key. Naming something a problem engenders the wrong relationship to it. It predetermines a pessimistic, already-defeated attitude. Try not to think of anything as a problem. Start with a forgiving relationship to laziness and impatience and cultivate a sense of humour about them both. And then trick them. Start a task or an activity *before* you are ready or after you are 'not ready'. For example, if you don't want to sit down and write, start to write before you can begin talking yourself out of it. Or, when impatient, slow down and speed up simultaneously. One foot presses the accelerator while, simultaneously, the other foot steps on the breaks.

The encounters with resistance and the compression of emotion generate one of the most crucial conditions for the theatre: energy. Energy is generated by the act of stepping up to bat; facing down the obstacle. An actor is only as successful as the quality of interaction with the emergent resistance of circumstance. The opposition between a force pushing towards action and another force holding back is translated into visible and feelable energy in space and time. This personal struggle with the obstacle in turn induces discord and imbalance. The attempt to restore harmony from this agitated state generates yet more energy. This battle is, in itself, the creative act.

It is natural and human to seek union and restore balance from the imbalance of engagement with discord. Recite an entire Shakespeare soliloquy from a physical state of imbalance. In the attempt to maintain equilibrium and not topple over while you speak, every part of your being reaches out for balance, harmony and union. This struggle is positive and productive. Suddenly the body speaks with astonishing clarity and necessity. The struggle requires precision and articulation.

⊂⊃

In 1991 I spent ten days as a guest of the Palestinians in Israel. As part of a small group of American theatre artists invited to look into the situation of Palestinian playwrights, actors and directors, we spent many, many hours talking with people in refuge camps and towns inside the Occupied Territories. It was exhausting. But I learned a great deal about resistance in the context of an entirely different political canvas.

In Israel and the Occupied Territories the problem is relatively clear: both sides want to live on the same piece of land. The repercussions of this existential fact devastate the daily lives of so many. In light of the ongoing adversity and degradation, I would have expected to see a population of Palestinians sitting in doorways with vacant eyes and lifeless shapes. But this was not the case at all. The awakeness and articulateness of the people we met and observed were astonishing to me. Their daily circumstances were so full of hardship and difficulty that I wondered what it was that prevented the Palestinians from giving up, capitulating in the face of the immense obstacles. I would have expected artistic expression to be a luxury. But in my travels in the West Bank and the Gaza Strip and in Israel itself, I met so many passionate and productive artists who bristled and expanded in the face of enormous impossibilities.

The Arabic word *Intifada*, which is the rubric for the Palestinian effort, is most often translated as 'resistance' but more accurate is 'shrugging off'. The word is an expression of a people rising up and shaking off the stigma under which they live. Even in the refugee camps I witnessed people who managed to become more awake and articulate under oppression rather than more numbed. I was impressed by the dignity and the political savvy of so many individuals in the refugee camps and towns. Despite the strict restrictions on renovation of housing, their modest living quarters were remarkably clean and well tended. Despite the restrictions on meeting anywhere in numbers that exceeded ten, people travelled from far and wide to see theatre hidden in basements.

This journey aroused in me my own responsibility to remain awake and articulate inside a very different political system at home. The parameters and rules are less visible and seemingly more benign than in the Middle East, but, in fact, are omnipresent and insidious in their capacity to generate numbness and collapse. We are the constant targets of huge commercial enterprises who have a great stake in our receptiveness and cooperation.

⬭

Theatre is the act of resistance against all odds. Art is a defiance of death. There will never be enough encouragement and support and we are all going to die. So why bother? Why put so much effort into a liminal activity? Why should we struggle so hard with a business that is at its heart only artifice?

Yale's *Theater Quarterly* asked me to contribute an article to an issue about utopia. At first I found it very difficult to think about the notion of utopia in relation to the theatre. I resisted thinking about utopia as some perfect, highly subsidized theatre palace of the future. I didn't want to consider how technology and theatre would intersect and become a new environment. Finally, in the heat of the writing deadline, I realized that utopia has nothing to do with the future. Utopia is now. The act of making theatre is already utopian because art is an act of resistance against circumstances. If you are making theatre now, you have already successfully achieved utopia.

Everything we do alters who we are. A great play offers the finest resistance to the theatre artist because it asks big questions and addresses critical human issues. Why choose a small play with minor themes? Why choose material you feel you can handle? Why not choose a play that is just beyond your reach? The reach is what changes you and gives your work energy and vitality.

I overheard a young director in technical rehearsals repeatedly ask an actor if he was comfortable. I finally had to ask him, 'Is the point of a rehearsal to be comfortable?' A good actor gets in the director's way. A good director gets in the actor's way. They set up purposeful resistances between them because differing perspectives serve to clarify the work at hand. Each has their own corresponding point of view: from the outside and from the inside; from the audience's experience and from the experience on the stage. The intention is to find flow and freedom through the mutual agreement to dissent.

And here is yet another paradox: you cultivate resistance in order to free your path of resistance. You welcome obstacles in order to find a way to annihilate them. The object is freedom.

In the fall of 1986 I watched the city of Paris close down for the entire day when Mikhail Gorbachev, the then President of the USSR, arrived for a visit with the President of France, Mitterrand. Traffic barricades throughout Paris made travel impossible between the airport and the palace where the two were to meet. In the late afternoon I sat in a café and watched Gorbachev's entourage sweep by me in a matter of milliseconds. Hundreds of thousands of Parisians had trouble getting around for a whole day so that one man's path could be freed of every hindrance.

I sat in the café astonished because, watching Gorbachev and his entourage pass by, I understood, for the first time, the meaning of power. Power is the elimination of obstacles. Power is speed. We all want to experience the charge of power that happens as all obstacles fly away, when words or actions pour out of us faster than we can think. The paradox is that we have to earn that speed and power and flow by embracing the obstacles until they evaporate.

Naturally we want freedom, flow and harmony in our work. These are qualities that give it eloquence. But we can not find this flow by avoiding the obstacles that arise upon starting out. We welcome the resistances and then apply our God-given ammunition – our imagination, energy and will – and finally watch the obstacles dissolve. Only then can we enjoy the new-found freedom and flow until the next obstacle appears. And the struggle begins anew. And hence, the paradox: we cultivate resistance in order to free our path of resistance. Real power is the removal of resistance from your path.

⊂⊃

The first time I saw Deborah Warner's production of T. S. Eliot's *The Waste Land*, performed by Fiona Shaw at the Dublin International Theatre Festival in 1995, I learned about another creative use of resistance. Although the play itself lasted only about half an hour, getting there was a trial. First it was very difficult to obtain tickets because so few were available to the general public. To accomplish the first task, getting a ticket to see the show, took time, effort and perseverance. Then Deborah Warner had insisted upon bringing audiences to a rather distant old fort which required special festival bus transportation from downtown Dublin. Once I managed to procure a ticket, I found my way to the part of town where two double-decker buses were scheduled to depart for the performance venue. Once inside the bus the audience had to wait for about forty-five minutes due to some technical difficulties at the performance space. Finally we headed out of town and presently the buses pulled up at the bottom of a steep hill below the site of the old fort. We exited the bus and were asked to wait once again in a field. Another half hour passed. For some reason the atmosphere was buoyant and no one seemed particularly annoyed at the delay. In fact, there was a feeling of expectation and adventure amongst us. After this final delay we walked up the hill and into an old barracks hall to experience Fiona Shaw and the intensely challenging T. S. Eliot's poem. The experience was quite simple and very extraordinary. There were no sound cues, no changing lights, not even any heat in the building. We, as an audience, were brought to a point that we might listen to an extraordinary woman speak this difficult text. The experience was wonderful. I felt prepared to listen. If the show had been done in a comfortable venue in town next to the other performance venues I do not believe that I would have been as present and receptive and listening. Doing the show downtown would have made the task of the theatre festival producers much easier. But Warner and Shaw had found the appropriate circumstances in which we might, together, experience something about *The Waste Land*. The resistances to experiencing it actually enhanced the listening and being.

About a year later I saw the production again, this time in Times Square in an old Broadway theatre just before it was to be renovated by Disney. Once again, although a completely different experience, it was a true one. Sitting within a decrepit environment, many seats covered with plastic, the cold winter night in the room with us, Warner and Shaw had found the proper resistances to share with a New York audience.

⸺

Your attitude towards resistance determines the success of your work and your future. Resistance should be cultivated. How you meet these obstacles that present themselves in the light of any endeavour determine the direction of your life and career.

Allow me to propose a few suggestions about how to handle the natural resistances that your circumstances might offer. Do not assume that you have to have some prescribed conditions to do your best work. Do not wait. Do not wait for enough time or money to accomplish what you think you have in mind. Work with what you have *right now*. Work with the people around you *right now*. Work with the architecture you see around you *right now*. Do not wait for what you assume is the appropriate, stress-free environment in which to generate expression. Do not wait for maturity or insight or wisdom. Do not wait till you are sure that you know what you are doing. Do not wait until you have enough technique. What you do *now*, what you make of your present circumstances will determine the quality and scope of your future endeavours.

And, at the same time, be patient.